Professional Machine Quilting

THE
COMPLETE
GUIDE TO
RUNNING A
SUCCESSFUL
QUILTING
BUSINESS

Carol A. Thelen

Martingale®
& COMPANY

Professional Machine Quilting: The Complete
Guide to Running a Successful Quilting Business

© 2003 by Carol A. Thelen

That Patchwork Place® is an imprint of Martingale
& Company®.

Martingale & Company
20205 144th Avenue NE
Woodinville, WA 98072-8478
www.martingale-pub.com

Printed in China
08 07 06 05 04 03   8 7 6 5 4 3 2 1

Credits

President . . . . Nancy J. Martin
CEO . . . . Daniel J. Martin
Publisher . . . . Jane Hamada
Editorial Director . . . . Mary V. Green
Managing Editor . . . . .Tina Cook
Technical Editor . . . . Karen Costello Soltys
Copy Editor . . . . Liz McGehee
Design Director . . . . Stan Green
Illustrator . . . . Laurel Strand
Text Designer . . . . Jennifer LaRock Shontz
Cover Designer . . . . Stan Green
Photographer . . . . Brent Kane

Mission Statement

*Dedicated to providing quality products
and service to inspire creativity.*

Library of Congress Cataloging-in-Publication Data

Thelen, Carol A.
   Professional machine quilting : the complete
guide to running a successful quilting business /
Carol A. Thelen.
      p. cm.
   ISBN 1-56477-509-7
   1. Machine quilting. 2. Small business—
Management. I. Title.
   TT835.T418 2003
   746.46'068—dc22
                                         2003016707

Contents

Introduction   4

CHAPTER 1
Is This Business Right for You? 6
Setting Goals ◆ Researching Your Market ◆ Estimating
Time and Income

CHAPTER 2
Expenses 13
Start-Up Costs ◆ Licenses, Fees, and Taxes ◆
Insurance ◆ Office Supplies ◆ Quilting Supplies

CHAPTER 3
Business Entities 25
Sole Proprietorship ◆ Partnership ◆ Corporation ◆
Limited Liability Company (LLC)

CHAPTER 4
Working at Home 27
Working in Solitude ◆ Child Care ◆ Household
Chores ◆ Working with Another Person ◆ Working
around Your Spouse ◆ Physical Concerns

CHAPTER 5
Setting Prices 31
Timing Chart ◆ Surface Area of a Quilt ◆ Recording
Data ◆ Batting ◆ Price Increases

CHAPTER 6
What Services Will You Offer? 40
Quilting ◆ Basting ◆ Binding ◆ Pressing Tops ◆
Backing ◆ Edge Basting ◆ Edge Trimming ◆ Quilt Labels

CHAPTER 7
Marketing 48
Quilt Shops ◆ Referrals and Fees ◆ Business Cards ◆
Brochures ◆ Local Marketing ◆ Internet ◆ Magazines ◆
Donations

CHAPTER 8
Developing Your Quilting Style 54
Classes and Videos ◆ International Machine Quilters
Association (IMQA) ◆ Internet E-Mail Lists ◆ Patterns
and Books ◆ Your Portfolio and Design Ideas

CHAPTER 9
Scheduling Your Time 57
Using a Calendar ◆ Scheduling Quilts ◆ Maintaining
a Waiting List ◆ Scheduling Clients ◆ Tracking Quilts
in Your Care

CHAPTER 10
Working with Clients 66
Your Reputation ◆ Telephone Checklist and
Journal ◆ Drop-Off Appointment ◆ Service Order ◆
Pick-Up Appointment ◆ Mail-Order Business ◆
Other Considerations

Resources 75

About the Author 78

Index 79

Introduction

So you want to stay home all day and quilt for other people? How nice to work for yourself, making money doing something you love. If you have never worked at home, the experience can be an eye-opener. You must be disciplined, organized, and motivated. You must wear many hats: accountant, supervisor, receptionist, quilter, janitor, repairman, purchaser, advertising manager, and more. All this in addition to the other hats you wear now: parent, spouse, homemaker, cook, chauffeur, caregiver, scout leader, landscaper, your other occupation, volunteer, and more.

I know the picture in your mind. You are happily quilting away watching those beautiful stitches first appear and then gently flow behind the needle. You're in a beautiful field of flowers with the wind gently blowing against your face. All is well and life is good! Then the thread breaks or tangles, or your high-speed, industrial hopping foot gets caught in a seam line that wasn't pieced correctly, or you realize that the line of stitching that took just two minutes to stitch in the wrong place will now take you three hours to rip out.

As you are ripping out all those stitches, the dryer is buzzing every two minutes, the phone rings, and you hear the school nurse leaving a message that your little Johnny needs to come home because he just got sick in Mrs. Periwinkle's first grade. This quilt needs to be finished when? Don't get caught up in the fantasy that your ideal business is quilting because it is your beloved hobby and passion. There is a fine line between the business of quilting for other people and the pleasure of making beautiful quilts for yourself. To keep your sanity and your passion for your hobby, you must define that line and carefully guard it.

I have a theory based on personal observation that many people start this business as a means to make extra money to pay for their quiltmaking hobby. As the word spreads of their quilting service and as their work gets better and better, their client list grows. The quiltmaker has now become a professional quilter. The business is successful, but with so many clients there is little or no time for making one's own quilts. The hobby no longer exists but has been replaced by a business. Lots of other quiltmakers are designing, piecing, and completing their quilts, hanging them in shows and giving them to friends and relatives. You, the professional quilter, have no quilts. If it is not your intention to stop making quilts for yourself, then don't let it happen. I fell into this rut and it took me about a year to realize what was happening. Since I was booked so far in advance, it took another year to do something about it! Keep your goals and your needs in mind, stay organized, and don't be afraid to say "No."

Always conduct yourself in a professional way. I refer to the people who bring me their quilt tops as clients, not customers. Merriam-Webster Online defines those two words as "customer: one that purchases a commodity or service," and "client: a person who engages the professional advice or services of another." The difference between these two definitions is *professional* and *advice*. You develop professional relationships with your clients because they come to trust your advice and the work you do.

This book is valuable to any professional quilter and focuses on the business of quilting—how to start it and how to be successful at it from a business point of view. It is written from the perspective that you are working alone with no quilting help from your spouse, family, or friends. If you do have help,

you are that much ahead of the game. The information concerning high-volume scheduling is directed to the professional who quilts more than one quilt top per week. If you quilt fewer than one top per week, your scheduling needs are just as important, although not as intense. Depending on the type of quilting you engage in (sit-down or stand-up machine) and the amount of time each quilt takes, as a professional quilter you can complete anywhere from one to a dozen or more quilts per week. Quilting a dozen quilts per week requires not only efficient use of lots of time but also precise scheduling and strict adherence to that schedule.

Now that I've pointed out the pitfalls of running a professional quilting business, let me assure you that my goal is not to scare you off. It's to make sure you're aware of all the issues you might face and that you're armed with the knowledge and tools you need to make your quilting business successful, without letting it overtake your life!

CHAPTER 1

Is This Business Right for You?

Before starting any business, dozens of questions need to be answered: legal, financial, and physical space concerns, to name a few. At times, you may wonder if you can actually make a quilting business work. In this chapter, we'll explore the possibility of your quilting service, to think about how it might fit into your daily life and how it might be used to fulfill the dream that you have envisioned. I'll touch briefly on some of the legal, tax, and financial issues; however, because these areas require the assistance of professionals in those fields, I mention them here only as something that you need to be aware of and that will require further research on your part.

Every business owner wants a high income with low expenses. As the owner and operator of a quilting service, time and money are interchangeable to you. Unless you have a computer-assisted machine or hire an employee, you make money only when you are quilting. The more time you spend quilting, the more money you make, so scheduling your time is important to your success. Once you've made the money, you can either invest it back into your business or keep it for yourself. You'll want to make informed decisions regarding any business purchase so you know you're getting a good value for your money and not wasting it (and thereby having less to keep as income for yourself). So, before you spend money on a business expense, ask yourself the following questions:

- Will it help me quilt faster or better?
- Will it free up some time that I can use for quilting?
- Can I get it cheaper somewhere else?
- Do I really need it?

Setting Goals

Before you dive into starting a business, there are plenty of things to take into consideration. You'll want to be sure that the business is what you're expecting it to be and that you realistically can dedicate the time required to make it work. If you have never been self-employed, there are many things to consider about working for yourself and working from your home. The most common questions about starting a quilting business include:

- How and where do I start?
- How much money can I really make?
- Won't it be wonderful to quilt for a living?

Start thinking about the goals and desires for your business and how you can fit them into your daily life. Do you want this business to pay for your quilting hobby or to supplement your retirement or family income? Perhaps you wish to quit your day job and you expect the quilting to replace that full-time income. Write down a wish list of all your goals. Brainstorm and put down anything and everything that comes to mind.

Use your wish list to stay on track or to remind you why you started this business in the first place. (Or to remind you why you didn't!) Look realistically at your goals and stay focused on the important things you want in life and from this business. Now that you have decided what you want, let's see how you can go about getting it.

Researching Your Market

Find out how many other quilting businesses are in your area. Many people have started in this business because, as quiltmakers looking for professional quilters to quilt their personal quilt tops, they discovered that the professional quilters in the area had very long waiting lists. If this is the case in your area, it's a good indication that work may be available to you.

Talk to the owner of your local shop. Perhaps you already have a relationship with the shop. If it doesn't offer quilting services, you can find out from the owner how many people call the shop asking for references for professional quilters. Ask if the shop would be willing to refer clients to you if you showed them samples of quality work. Some shop owners will be willing to keep your cards and brochures at the counter.

Occasionally, we hear of not-so-healthy relationships between professional quilters and quilt-shop owners. Some shop owners may be unwilling to establish a relationship with a professional quilter because they might see the quilter as taking business away from them. One example would be if you were to sell every type of batting offered by the quilt shop. Perhaps you can compromise and sell a brand or two of batting that the quilt shop doesn't carry. Convince the owner that having a professional quilter nearby means that their customers can complete more quilts. They can shop for fabric for their next project while their current one is off being quilted.

Estimating Time and Income

It is possible to make a living being a professional quilter, but your success will depend on three things: how much time you put into your business, how much you charge per quilt, and how many quilts you complete. These three variables are hard to control and difficult to predict. In this section we'll try to get at least some idea about the income you might expect based on the time you have available. Can you quit your nine-to-five job? No one can answer this question but you. Unless you can afford to live without your present salary, don't quit your current job! It is best to ease into a professional quilting business gradually; see how you like running the business and work toward someday quitting that job.

In the discussions that follow, I give you hour and dollar figures that are loosely based on my actual experience using a long-arm quilting machine. At several times in my quilting career I kept track of the actual time it took me to complete certain quilting tasks. These times and tasks were combined to give me rough ideas of time and money for my business based on the prices I charged at the time. Use these examples as you go through the process of estimating your possible annual income from quilting. It is in no way intended that you use these figures as hard-and-fast costs or fees to determine if you should start a quilting business. These exercises are intended to give you equations to use with your own figures. After reading through the examples, you will fill in the numbers that pertain to your situation, so be honest with yourself and proceed with caution.

In this process, we make some estimates or assumptions:

◆ Time you have available each week to invest in your quilting business

◆ Number of quilts you might complete in that time
◆ Average dollar amount you might expect to receive for each quilt
◆ Average income you might receive each week that you work
◆ Number of weeks you actually work each year
◆ Annual income

TIME

Now that you have listed your business goals, let's find out when you have the time available to achieve them. Start by looking at the things that need to be done in your life, such as shopping for groceries, cooking meals, cleaning house, taking children to their activities, or caring for elderly parents or other relatives with special needs. Do you have a full-time job? Do you have commitments at your house of worship, your quilt guild, or your garden club? Do you want to continue to make quilts for yourself? Do you exercise regularly, do you need to get plenty of sleep at night, and do you like to take short rest breaks?

For this exercise, you need a weekly calendar. I like one that shows a week at a time with a column for each day divided into quarter- or half-hour increments from 8 A.M. to 7 P.M. You are going to take a realistic look at all the things you do each week and write them in this calendar.

Write down all the things you have to do and all the things you would like to do: chores and errands, meetings, doctor appointments, hair appointments, kids' ball games, dinner with your spouse, guild meetings, and anything else that you know of for now. If your guild meets once each month on the first Monday, fill in that day for the entire year. If you know you go for your annual checkup in July of each year, fill that in for the first week of July and revise it when you have the actual appointment date. When possible, try to schedule tasks such as meetings, doctor appointments, and grocery shopping on one day. That will leave larger blocks of time open on other days in the week for quilting.

Next, find out if any time is left in your week to run a quilting business. Fill in blocks of time where you would be able to quilt and run your business. Frequent stopping and starting adds more time to complete each project, so if you can get uninterrupted sessions of at least one hour, that's better. If all you have is 15 or 30 minutes, however, then schedule that time as well. If you plan to work evenings, at night, or on weekends, schedule those times as quilting times. This is *your* schedule and you should complete it in accordance with your lifestyle and your work habits.

Of the times scheduled for quilting, include time for scheduling appointments with clients. When I first started in my business, I would schedule appointments all through the week. I found that I was not getting any quilting done because appointments chopped up my time. When I started scheduling appointments on specific days of the week, things went much more smoothly. Here is an example of how I schedule my time:

◆ Monday is for bill paying and errand running so all these errands and interruptions are on one day instead of spread out over the entire week. If I get done early, I use the extra time for quilting, paperwork, or for myself.

◆ Tuesday and Wednesday are quilting days between the hours of 9 A.M. and 4 P.M. This gives me time to get the kids off to school and to fit in my daily exercise. I stop at 4 o'clock to cook dinner and meet the kids when they come home from school. In a perfect world, these two days give me 14 hours of pure quilting time—key word here being "perfect."

◆ Thursday and Friday are client drop-off and pick-up days. The time between appointments is used for quilting or household chores or sometimes both. Depending on the number of appointments scheduled in a week, I might be able to fit in an additional seven hours or so of quilting on these days.

◆ Saturday and Sunday are generally for family time—and my own piecing or quilting.

Using my weekly schedule as an example, you see that my quilting times are 14 hours total on Tuesday and Wednesday plus another 7 hours on Thursday and Friday. That gives me 21 hours of quilting time each week if I don't want to quilt in the evenings or on the weekends. You can already see that, in this example, this business is a part-time endeavor.

Fill in your calendar and be honest with yourself. If you know you won't quilt after 9 P.M. or you won't be able to quilt very long when the kids are home, then don't schedule that as quilting time. After you've filled in several weeks of your calendar, determine the number of hours you can devote to your quilting business. Use that number as we go on to the next part of this exercise. I will use my total of 21 hours per week in the following examples.

QUILTS PER WEEK

Now that you have blocked out times for your quilting business and you have a general idea of the time you can devote to it, let's look at how long it takes to complete one quilt. After estimating the time it takes to complete the "average" quilt, you'll have a rough idea of the number of quilts you can complete in your workweek.

Keep in mind that it can take anywhere from 2 to 10 hours (or more) of actual quilting time to complete one quilt. That doesn't include the time it takes to talk to the client and schedule the appointment, conduct the appointment, prepare the invoice, call when the quilt is ready, schedule another appointment for pick up of the completed quilt, or do the paperwork. As a very rough average, let's say that each quilt takes 7 hours to complete. Depending on the type and amount of quilting and the quilting system you use, this number will be more or less. For the purposes of this example I'll use 7 hours, which does include all the associated paperwork and appointments.

Using 7 hours per quilt and 21 hours per week, this means I can complete three quilts per week in my schedule: 21 available hours ÷ 7 hours per quilt = 3 quilts per week.

Determine how many quilts you can realistically complete in one week using your estimates. If you already have a good estimate of how long it takes you to complete a quilt, use that number here. If not, make your best estimate of how long it will take you to quilt a queen-size quilt with a moderate amount of quilting. To that figure add about two hours for client meetings and paperwork.

AVERAGE DOLLAR AMOUNT OF EACH QUILT

There is no such thing as an "average price per quilt" that will fit all quilters. Each professional quilter can determine the average price he or she makes per quilt over a certain time period by collecting and analyzing the data. In the past, I have kept data on the number of quilts I completed, the time it took me to complete those quilts, and the amount of money I received for the quilting. Over time, I was able to come up with an average dollar amount per quilt. You need to determine what an average dollar amount per quilt might be for your business.

If there are other professional quilters in your area, find out what they charge for quilting. Some charge per square inch, per square foot, or per square yard; others have a range of prices for a range of quilt sizes. Prices vary for different types of quilting, too. Using a quilt that is 75" x 95" as an example and the prices you are quoted by the quilters in your area, determine what it would cost you to have this top quilted by these quilters.

The table on the facing page lists several fictional rates for quilting services. The 75" x 95" quilt is equivalent to 7125 square inches, 49.5 square feet, or 5.5 square yards. These units represent the surface area of the quilt top, and all are commonly used to determine quilting fees.

Listed under the Rate column are several different fictional rates that might be charged by quilters. The dollar figures are calculated by multiplying the rate by the surface area. Example: $0.03/square inch x 7125 square inches = $213.75.

Make a chart like the one on the facing page using the various rates quoted by quilters in your area. Note the differences in pricing structure and quilting fees. Which structure makes more sense to you and which prices seem reasonable to you? My personal preference is to charge by the square yard because quilters are already familiar with a price per yard of 42"-wide fabric. A square yard is slightly smaller than the surface area of one yard of fabric.

Using the prices in the chart, let's find an average cost per quilt. Add all the dollar totals together to get $849.07. Divide that number by 7 (the number of different price quotes) to come up with an average income per quilt of $121.29.

FEE DATA			
Rate	7125 Square Inches	49.5 Square Feet	5.5 Square Yards
$ 0.01/square inch	$71.25		
$ 0.02/square inch	$142.50		
$ 0.03/square inch	$213.75		
$ 1.35/square foot		$66.82	
$ 2.50/square foot		$123.75	
$16.00/square yard			$88.00
$26.00/square yard			$143.00

Use the numbers from your chart to determine the average income per quilt. If your chart has only three prices, total those three prices and divide by three to get the average income per quilt.

AVERAGE INCOME PER WEEK

So far in our example, we have determined that a total of 21 hours per week can be devoted to a quilting business and that three quilts can be completed in this week. Now we have estimated that the average income per quilt is $121. For one week of quilting, the income from three quilts is: 3 x $121 = $363. Use the numbers from your charts and calendars to find your estimated income per week.

NUMBER OF WORKWEEKS

Now you need to estimate the number of weeks per year that you want to work. Do you like to take long vacations? Attend quilt shows and classes out of town? Take holiday breaks? Be realistic in determining how many full weeks per year you will actually work. At the very least, subtract 5 weeks from the 52 weeks per year. If you had a "regular" job, you would get about 10 days worth of holidays and about 2 weeks of vacation days. Take off another 5 days for sick days and that leaves you with 5 weeks off per year. For your business, that leaves 47 workweeks per year (52 - 5 = 47).

ANNUAL INCOME

To estimate your annual income, multiply the number of workweeks by the estimated income per week. The estimated annual income in our sample quilting business is: 47 weeks x $363 per week = $17,061 annual income.

That total is gross annual income from quilting only and your expenses are deducted from this amount. If you offer other services and products such as batting, binding, or piecing, you can add the profits from those products and services. Remember, if you add other services such as piecing or binding, you must schedule time to complete them. The services that are not part of the quilting take time away from your actual quilting time.

How do your numbers look to you? Do you need more time to quilt? Should you charge more money per quilt or offer more products and services? This exercise is designed to show you how time and money are interchangeable in your business. If you are not happy with the numbers you see, your options are to find more time to quilt or to raise the prices. In my example schedule, I pay for the services of a housecleaner. She can do in three hours what takes me six hours to do—and she does a better job. (I hate housework!) I look at the six hours she saves me as six hours in which I can complete a quilt or do personal things. I can pay her out of the income from the quilt and still have some left over, so we are both making money. Look for ways to free up more time that you can devote to your business or family.

CHAPTER 2

Expenses

When you are just starting out, you might feel you need everything all at once. Resist the temptation to purchase anything until you know you need it. There are things you need right away, things that can wait, and things you might never need or want. Start-up expenses can be high, so do your research before spending money.

In this section I explain some expenses you might incur. As you go through each expense, make a list of the things you need right away and the things that can wait. I base my buying decisions on one thing: money. Will the item pay for itself by saving me time or money? Will the item make me money? Can I get a comparable product somewhere else cheaper? If the item enables me to quilt faster or better, how long will it take to pay for itself? Try not to make impulse purchases. You might regret them later.

Start-Up Costs

Your start-up costs will depend on your individual situation. As you read through this section, take note of the things you might need and seek out estimates of those costs. These things might include:

◆ Attorney and accountant fees for setting up legal and financial records and record-keeping systems

◆ Filing fees, permits, bank accounts, and license fees

◆ Costs for preparing your studio

◆ Costs for leasing office or retail space, including rent, utilities, and insurance

◆ Cost for machines, classes, supplies, and advertising

◆ Office expenses, such as telephone, calculator, computer, and filing system

As you go through the process of planning your business, keep a list of items you'll need and their costs. The key is to try to keep your costs to a minimum. Make a list of office supplies you need and check to make sure you don't already have them at home before going to the office-supply store. Begin keeping records and receipts of all the expenses you incur, even while you are just deciding whether or not to start a business. If you travel to a dealer, quilt shop, or office-supply store, keep track of the mileage and travel costs. Any reference books, office supplies, accounting books or software, and such are tax-deductible if you open your business in that year.

If you are securing a loan for start-up costs, your financial institution might require a business plan. Ask your loan officer what information the bank requires in the plan or look to your financial institution, local library, or bookstore for books that offer guidance in writing business plans if you need one.

BUSINESS MILEAGE RECORDS

It is important to keep a written record of your business mileage. It is a question on the IRS tax form. I keep a small monthly pocket calendar in my car to record mileage. At the end of each month I total the mileage, and then at the end of the year I total the 12 months. At the beginning of the year (or when you begin recording your business mileage), record the odometer reading of the car you are using and do the same at the end of the year. The IRS will want to know the mileage totals for business, commuting, and personal trips.

Many government agencies offer free advice and publications about starting and running your own business. Keep the business plan simple but be sure to include all the information required by your financial institution. Some of the requirements for a business plan include start-up and ongoing costs and potential income. The potential income for your business is covered in "Estimating Time and Income" on page 8.

Licenses, Fees, and Taxes

Here we talk about possible taxing entities and what tax burdens you might incur in your business. Generally, on the local level, you might need a permit to open or operate your business. The state might want sales and/or use taxes as well as income taxes. In addition, some states may require you to pay franchise or other business taxes. The federal government, of course, will want federal income taxes.

The type and amount of taxes, business permits, and license fees you are required to pay depend on where you live, how big your business is, and what type of business entity you set up. Your certified public accountant (CPA), attorney, or state and local government agencies can help you with gathering information and filing the necessary paperwork.

One of my students, Holly Heath, shared with me a Web site address that lists virtually every taxing or governmental agency by state. Use this Web site as a starting point when researching agencies applicable to your location: www.statelocalgov.net.

WHOLESALE VERSUS RETAIL AND SALES AND USE TAXES

Generally, the wholesale price of a product is half of the retail price. One common misconception is that if you own a business or have a federal or state tax ID number from your state, you are entitled to purchase anything for your business at wholesale cost and not pay tax on it. This is not entirely true. When a product goes from a manufacturer to a consumer, it generally is bought and sold several times. The only time the sale of the product becomes a taxable event is when the actual consumer buys it. Here's why:

When a manufacturer purchases supplies used to make a product, they do not pay sales tax. The manufacturer makes the product and generally sells very large quantities to a distributor, who pays less than wholesale for the product. Since the distributor is purchasing the product to resell to someone else, the purchase price is not taxable.

Now the distributor has large quantities of the product and needs to resell it to someone else. The distributor's customers are called retailers. Retailers are the professional quilters, quilt shops, grocery stores, department stores, and the like. Retailers purchase products in moderate quantities from distributors and pay the wholesale price. Since the retailer is purchasing the product to resell to someone else, again the sale is not taxable. When a customer walks into a store and purchases the product, they are buying it to use, not to resell. This is when the sale of that product becomes a taxable event.

How does this all relate to your business? Consider that you'll offer batting. You purchase it from a distributor in a large quantity for the purpose of reselling to your clients. You are charged wholesale prices for the batting and do not pay sales tax on your purchase. You are exempt from the sales tax because you are reselling it to your client. Since they are the end users of the batting, you will need to charge them sales tax (provided your state has a sales tax).

Some distributors or manufactures might sell products to you at wholesale or below retail cost; however, if you are going to use those products and not resell them, you are required to pay taxes on them. Items for charity are generally exempt from these taxes. Sellers can incur large fines if they do not properly collect required sales or use taxes. When you purchase items for resale or items that are tax-exempt, the seller will ask for a tax ID number, a resale certificate, or other proof required by the state.

FEDERAL TAXES

Any business or person who makes an income is required to file a federal income-tax return. The IRS form you use depends on the type of business entity you set up for yourself. The simplest IRS form to use is Schedule C, which is an attachment to your personal income-tax form. Others include partnership forms and corporation forms, and they can become quite confusing, which is why a CPA can be a valuable asset. CPAs offer many services, from simple advice about setting up or keeping accounting records to completing your entire tax return. You may think a CPA is an unnecessary expense, but in my opinion, the fees are a small price to pay for knowing you have your financial records in order.

Save records or receipts of all business transactions and keep them filed in an organized manner. Staying organized throughout the year pays off when it comes time to prepare your tax returns, and it will also help if you are ever audited.

STATE TAXES

Most states require retail and service businesses to collect the sales and/or use taxes that I discussed above. You will need to register for a tax number and permit with your state revenue or comptroller's office; most states do not require a fee for this. You collect these taxes from your clients and you pay them to the state monthly, quarterly, or yearly. Generally the more taxes you collect, the more frequently you are required to file. In addition to collecting sales tax, many businesses are subject to state income or other taxes. Check with your state for its requirements.

COUNTY AND CITY PERMITS

You may be required to obtain a business permit or license from your county, parish, city, or town. If you are operating your business from home, check the deed restrictions and zoning requirements for your city or neighborhood. Many subdivisions and some cities do not allow you to use your home for your business. Usually this prohibition is in place to keep vehicular traffic out of a neighborhood or to keep large business trucks and vans from parking overnight on neighborhood streets and in driveways.

Some restrictions may be less stringent, stating merely how large a business sign can be or how many buildings you can erect on your property.

If you are leasing or purchasing space or a building for business use, check for business restrictions on that particular space or property. Often cities change building codes or ordinances, so before you can be issued a permit to open your business you will need to bring the property up to current code. It can be quite expensive if you need to brick the front entrance, add landscaping, or add bathrooms or parking spaces for the disabled. Before you sign a lease or a mortgage, make sure the property is up to code or that you negotiate with the present owner regarding who will be responsible to make and pay for the required improvements.

Insurance

Check with your insurance agent about business insurance to cover your equipment and your liability. Rules and regulations can vary between states or between insurance companies within a state. Your best source for information is your insurance agent. Here are some questions to ask your agent:

- ◆ Am I covered if a client trips and injures herself on my property?
- ◆ Are my quilting machine, sewing machines, supplies, and furniture covered for fire, theft, wind, and rising water? Note: Only the federal government writes flood insurance, but you can purchase it through your insurance agent.
- ◆ Are my clients' quilts covered if they are damaged or stolen while in my care?

Take an inventory of all your business and personal assets and total up the costs. With quilting systems costing $10,000 to $15,000 or even more, you might be required to purchase an addendum or rider to your homeowner's policy.

To lower your insurance costs, try the following:

◆ Shop around to find the best deal.

◆ Use one insurance agent for all your insurance needs, including auto, home, flood, life, and business. Usually you can get discounts if you have one agent for all your insurance. If your agent doesn't mention a discount, be sure to ask.

◆ Ask your agent about other ways to lower your premiums, such as installing alarm systems, deadbolt locks, fire extinguishers, carbon-monoxide alarms, and smoke alarms. Even if you don't get an insurance discount for these items, you should strongly consider purchasing smoke detectors and fire extinguishers for your home and quilting studio.

◆ Raise your deductible. Your annual insurance premiums will be lower, but if you make a claim, you'll need to pay more out of pocket before your insurance coverage kicks in.

◆ Ask about other discounts, too, even if they don't relate to your business insurance. Senior citizens, drivers with good records, and even students with good grades may be eligible for auto-insurance discounts.

Office Supplies

You'll need basic office supplies to keep records and run your business efficiently.

Files and filing system. When I file federal income tax for my business, I use Schedule C. To make it easier at tax time, I use a filing system that mimics the items listed on this form. An expanding file with tabs and dividers works well. Check with your CPA about setting up and keeping your records.

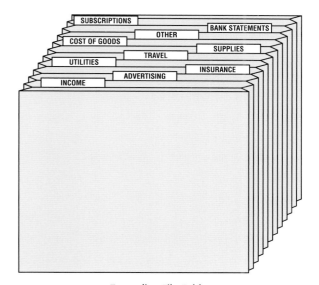

Expanding File Folder

Computer, scanner, printer. You can use this equipment to produce your own business cards, brochures, invoices, patterns, and forms as well as to keep records. Access to the Internet is important for sharing information with quilters around the world and for communicating with clients near and far. You can use a scanner to resize quilting patterns.

Telephone and Internet access. Consider getting a second line for your business. If you want Internet access, you can choose a low-cost, dial-up account or a high-speed, always-on connection. The faster the information comes into and out of your computer, the higher the cost. Read the fine print before signing up for telephone or Internet service. You might be locking yourself into a contract for a year or more and it might impose considerable charges for early termination.

As an alternative to a second phone line, you might consider a cellular phone for your business. The cost can be much lower than a second phone line, and many cellular packages come with other useful features, such as voice mail and call forwarding.

Answering machine or caller ID. These are essential in your business because interruptions waste time, costing you money. Use an answering system to take messages, and return calls at certain times during the day. If you work from home, an answering system allows you to set and keep business hours. An alternative to an answering machine is voice mail from your phone company. When your business is "closed," your clients can leave a message that you can return during your next business hours. Having caller ID on a cordless phone puts the phone nearby and tells you who is calling. You can take the calls you want and let the answering machine get the calls you'll return later.

Checking accounts, credit cards, and merchant accounts. It is desirable—and required for some business entities—to keep business and personal records separate. Shop around for the best bank-account and credit-card rates. Some banks charge a fee for each business deposit and/or withdrawal. If you must use a credit card to make purchases for your business, pay the balance due each month to avoid finance charges. Credit-card interest rates are high, and the quicker you pay them off, the more money stays in your pocket.

You'll need a merchant account if you plan to accept credit cards for payment. Merchant account fees can add up quickly: statement fees each month, a fee for each transaction, and a percentage of each sale. In my experience, I have only had several clients ask if I accept credit cards. Unless you have an extremely high volume of credit-card sales, a merchant account is an expense you don't need.

Bookkeeping software or books. Your accounting system doesn't need to be elaborate, just accurate and easy to maintain. Keep records of your income and expenses and, if you purchase goods for sale, keep track of your inventory. A simple spread sheet or accounting journal can be purchased at an office-supply store. These journals have columns for income and expenses, and generally you total them up each week or month. A sales receipt book with duplicate pages keeps track of your income and provides your client with a receipt.

Bookkeeping software might save a little time. The software I recommend is Quicken Home and Business because you can use it to keep both personal and business records and to prepare and print invoices. Similar software is sometimes available when you purchase a new computer. Another program that keeps track of time for each project as well as inventory is QuickBooks or QuickBooks Pro. All of these programs are available from Intuit (see "Resources" on page 75).

Quilting Supplies

As you read through the list of quilting supplies below, think about how and where you can store them in your studio. Add the cost of any storage items, such as bookshelves or tables, to your list of expenses.

LIGHTING

Proper lighting is essential in your studio. Choose overhead florescent lighting or floor lamps that light up the entire studio space. The older we get, the more light we need, so don't skimp on the light sources.

QUILT STORAGE

Quilt tops and backing waiting to be quilted should be properly stored. The storage system you select should keep the fabric and batting clean and dry as well as free from dust and smoke. Keep the number of tops waiting to be quilted to a minimum. This cuts down on the storage space needed and means less liability for you should something happen to quilt tops in your care. I like to keep no more than two weeks worth of tops waiting to be quilted or of finished quilts waiting for pickup. I store quilt tops in the same jumbo, brown paper bags with twisted handles that I use to package completed quilts I am returning to clients. Some examples of storage ideas include open shelving, cubed storage bins, or large, see-through plastic containers.

SPARE PARTS AND TOOLS

Spare machine parts are essential for keeping your business going. Often, some small, inexpensive part can bring your productivity to a standstill. If you keep a supply of spare parts on hand, you can simply replace the part and continue with your quilting. Ask your dealer which spare parts he recommends that you keep on hand, and order them with the machine. Generally, home sewing–machine parts can be purchased from your nearby dealer, but parts for your stand-up quilting system might need to be ordered and shipped, taking extra days. Below are some critical parts to keep on hand.

Timing tool. Every long-arm quilter should know how to time his or her machine, and some dealers and suppliers sell a special tool used to quickly time the machine. Ask your dealer to show you how to time your machine, or refer to the instructions for timing a machine in my book *Long-Arm Machine Quilting* (Martingale & Company, 2002).

If you are quilting with your home sewing machine or with a short-arm machine, your dealer most likely will recommend that you not adjust the timing. Check with your dealer for his or her advice.

Screwdrivers and Allen wrenches. Manufacturers supply you with some of the tools needed to service the machine and replace needles. You'll need a medium-size screwdriver to unscrew the throat plate and time the machine. A small screwdriver or Allen wrench is needed to adjust the bobbin tension, change needles, and change foot attachments.

Check springs. Check springs are part of the tension device. This spring gets a workout each time the needle is raised and lowered. The constant movement of this bit of thin metal over time causes it to fatigue and break.

Switches. Usually there are four switches on the handles of long-arm and short-arm machines. It is not unusual for a switch to fail over time. In a pinch, you can move a working switch to replace the failed switch until a replacement arrives. But it's a good idea to have at least one spare switch on hand.

Emery cord. Emery cord is a thin, abrasive cord used to smooth out burrs in metal parts. Burrs are caused by the needle hitting another metal part, and they can cut the thread. The easiest way to smooth out burrs in small, hard-to-get-to areas is to use emery cord.

NOTIONS

The more you quilt, the faster you'll use up or wear out critical notions such as needles, pins, and bobbins.

Needles. Keep a supply of machine and hand-sewing needles so you can change them often.

Bobbins and bobbin case. If you are not using prewound bobbins, you'll need a large supply of bobbins. The more thread types or colors you keep in stock, the more bobbins you'll need. Consider buying about 25 bobbins at a minimum. If you use prewound bobbins, you can keep fewer of the refillable bobbins on hand.

The bobbin case holds the bobbin during sewing. The tension screw on the bobbin case is used to make tension adjustments to the bobbin thread. Different types of threads require different tensions. Instead of adjusting the tension for a particular thread, some quilters prefer to have a preset bobbin case for each type of thread they use, making thread changes quick and easy.

Pins and scissors. Every quilter should have a supply of all-purpose pins, such as yellow-head straight pins, for general use. For pinning tops and backings to canvas leaders, you'll need some long, strong pins. Florist pins, which can be purchased at discount stores, have large pearl heads that are easy to grasp while pinning and unpinning, and the long, sturdy shafts hold up well when pinned through several layers of fabric and canvas.

You'll need to have several pairs of scissors on hand. Use a small pair of blunt-end scissors to clip threads while quilting. The blunt end is less likely to accidentally clip the fabric when you're clipping threads. Choose scissors that are lightweight and easy to handle. For trimming the edges of completed quilts, use a pair of large, sharp scissors, such as dressmaking shears.

One way to keep track of your thread-clipping scissors is with a retractable scissors holder. This gadget pins or clips to your clothing and has a spring-loaded cord that clips to your scissors handle. Take care when using one, because if you let go of the scissors when the cord is fully extended, the scissors may retract into your face at a high speed.

SEWING MACHINE

If you plan to offer piecing, seaming, backing, or binding services, you'll need a good sewing machine with an accurate ¼" presser foot and a walking foot for attaching the bindings. A cone adapter allows you to use economical cone thread on your regular sewing machine.

CUTTING AND PRESSING TOOLS

A rotary cutter with a sharp blade (and a packet of replacement blades), a cutting ruler, and a cutting mat are needed for squaring up backings, trimming uneven edges, and cutting strips for binding. For pressing seams, quilt tops, backings, and bindings, you'll need a good iron and a large ironing surface—and ready access to them. If you use a steam iron, you'll also need distilled water or access to tap water, depending on your iron.

Cutting and pressing surfaces should be large enough to hold yards of fabric. An inexpensive, combined cutting and pressing surface can be made from a hollow-core door. Cover one end of the door with batting and muslin and then staple them to the underside of the door to make a pressing surface; the other end is used for the cutting mat. Place the door on top of cabinets or file drawers so it is at the right height for you. Inexpensive, plastic drawer units for this purpose can be purchased at discount or office-supply stores. Not only do you have a cutting and pressing surface but you have storage as well. For comfort while standing, the height should be 3" below your elbow when it is bent at 90°. Help your posture and prevent backaches while standing by putting one foot up on a stool or step as you cut or press.

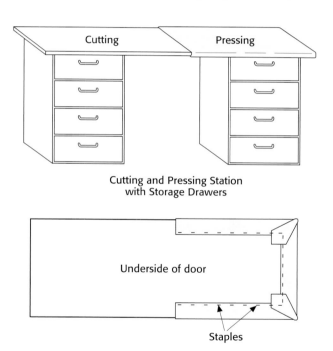

Cutting and Pressing Station
with Storage Drawers

BATTING

If you choose to sell batting as part of your business, you will need storage space for the rolls or packages. Rolls of batting are more economical than packages and can be stored upright on the floor or hung from a holder. Most long-arm quilting systems have a batting holder mounted under the table. A 12-foot table can store one roll of batting that is as wide as 126", or two rolls of 96"-wide batting that have been

folded and rolled; a 14-foot table can hold three of these rolls. Packaged battings can be stored on shelves or in large bins.

If you sell several types of batting,
you can store them upright on the floor.

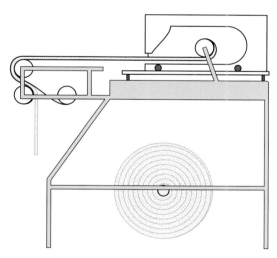

You can also store batting on a holder
under the quilting table.

Limit your batting choices to one or two types that you like to use and that sell well for you. Any type of batting that sits in your studio for a long time is not making money for you, so don't reorder it once it has been used up.

THREAD

If you don't use prewound bobbins, consider purchasing two cones or spools of the same color and type of thread—one for the machine and one for the bobbin winder. You can save time by keeping the sewing cone on the machine while the bobbin cone is winding.

Store thread in a drawer, closet, or cabinet so it is out of direct sunlight and away from dust. Wooden cone holders can hang on a wall or sit on a counter for easy access, but be careful about light and dust. Large plastic containers with lids hold a great deal of thread. However you choose to store your thread, make sure it's in an easily accessible place so clients are able to choose their colors.

Cotton or polyester. When you are just starting your business, the issue of thread can be confusing and expensive. Start with samples of different threads to find the brand and type that sews well for you and looks good in the quilt. Polyester and cotton-covered polyester threads tend to be stronger than all-cotton thread, making them good threads for high-speed machines and beginning quilters. Many brands of cotton thread are less forgiving for beginners, but they are good threads. A small supply of thread is usually included with the purchase of a machine. If samples are not available, choose neutral colors of different brands to try while you are learning.

Once you have decided which thread to offer, you'll need a variety of colors when you begin taking in quilts. Some commonly used colors are white, black, navy, Christmas red, and hunter green. Some neutrals include eggshell or muslin, "tea-dyed" muslin, and dark gray. The tea-dyed muslin color is darker than regular muslin so it blends in better with medium to dark fabrics. Dark gray is lighter than black and tends to blend in better than black thread with medium to dark fabrics.

Monofilament. Depending on the manufacturer, this type of thread is made from either nylon or polyester. It typically comes in clear and smoke "colors." When using monofilament, use a cotton or polyester thread that matches the quilt backing in the bobbin. Take care when securing stitches because this thread unsews itself more easily than other threads.

Decorative threads. A large variety of decorative threads can be used in your quilting machine. Two things that are important to consider when choosing decorative threads are colorfastness and strength. *Colorfast* means that the colors won't run and they resist fading. Check for guaranteed colorfastness by the manufacturer. Decorative threads also need to be strong enough to run at high speeds through your machine. Polyester threads made for embroidery machines are a good choice because they are designed for use on industrial, high-speed machines, while rayon threads break more often.

ACCESSORIES AND STITCHING TOOLS

Stitch guides, rulers, stencils, and templates are all tools of the professional machine quilter. These tools are great time-savers, and the number of tools available seems to grow rapidly. While their sizes vary in width and length, these types of tools are usually relatively thin, so a large drawer about 4" deep is a good place to store them. I use a 17" x 17" zippered vinyl tote to store all my rulers and templates.

COMFORT AIDS

Floor pads help reduce the stress of standing all day on a hard surface. Interlocking, foam floor pads are available at warehouse stores and home-improvement centers. Sitting for long periods can be stressful as well. Choose an adjustable chair with good support for your back and arms if you sit down to quilt.

DISPLAY STAND

When clients come to pick up their completed quilts, it's nice to be able to display the quilt properly. One way to do this without taking up too much space is to use a photographer's backdrop stand. You can purchase one where professional camera equipment is sold or on the Internet (see "Resources" on page 75). These stands are made of three pieces: two legs and a crossbar. Each leg piece stands alone on a tripod and can extend as high as the ceiling. The crossbar extends to the width of a king-size quilt. It telescopes into itself for easy storage.

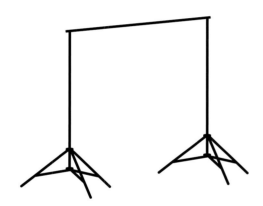

Photographer's Backdrop Stand

Use clip-on curtain rings (available from a discount store) to hang the quilt in lieu of a hanging sleeve. Be sure the rings are large enough to fit around the crossbar. A photographer's stand will enable you to display an entire quilt and, at the same time, keep it out of your work area. Clients are proud to see their quilts hanging. Many of my return clients bring their cameras to the pick-up appointment to take advantage of an opportunity to photograph the displayed quilt.

Clip-On Curtain Ring

GET ORGANIZED!

During my first year in business, I spent all my profits on every tool and gadget available. I had no idea what I had or where it was. Several years later, I decided to do a complete cleaning of my studio and clear out things I was no longer using or had never used. I was amazed at some of the things I found.

Keep an inventory of your business assets—such as rotary cutters, rulers, mats, needles, spare parts, computers, and irons—so you know what you have. Not only does an inventory save you money by preventing duplicate purchases, but it is also important to have for insurance purposes.

CAMERA

Many of the quilts you complete will leave your studio never to be seen again, so it is a good idea to take pictures while you can. Document them and keep them in a photo album. Take photos of whole quilts as well as close-ups of your quilting. Your album can provide inspiration for future quilts and will be a good way to show samples of your work to prospective clients.

If you are taking a lot of pictures, you might consider purchasing a high-quality digital camera. In the long run, the cost of the digital camera may be less than the expense of processing film. You can store the pictures on your computer and print out only those that you want to keep in the album. Use quality photo paper to print pictures to show clients. Another advantage of going digital is that you can see the picture before the quilt leaves your possession instead of waiting to have film developed and potentially being disappointed with the shot.

QUILT BAGS

Once you have completed a quilt, you'll need to put it in a bag or other carrier for the client. Don't use plastic garbage bags unless the bags are clear. I've heard horror stories of quilts in these garbage bags being taken out to the curb and delivered to the landfill. Check your discount or warehouse store for the clear plastic bags.

Some alternatives to plastic bags are paper or plastic shopping bags with handles or drapery hangers with covers. I use the jumbo, kraft-paper bags with twisted handles. They hold the largest king-size quilts, stand up nicely, and are easy to carry.

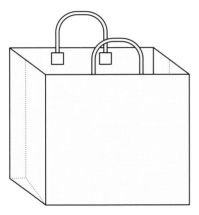

Jumbo, Kraft-Paper Bag

PAPERWORK

Keeping up with household paperwork is work enough, without the extra burden of business paperwork. Take a little time each day to pay business and personal bills and to enter accounting records for home and business. To save time, make it your policy to never let a piece of paper cross your desk more than once.

When the mail arrives, throw out (or recycle) the junk and take care of the rest. The rest can include bank statements, bills, and other papers that need further attention. If the bills and bank statements will be tended to later when you are scheduled to do paperwork, put them in a temporary file marked "Bills to Pay." Later, on paperwork day, pay the bills or reconcile the bank statements or whatever else needs to be done, and then file the papers in their permanent files.

CHAPTER 3

Business Entities

The type of business entity you establish has an effect on how you are taxed and on how you can borrow money. It also determines your personal financial liabilities. The choices covered in this chapter apply to U.S. businesses only. If you live in another country, you'll need to check with your local authorities regarding the appropriate type of business entity for you. Even if you are a U.S. resident, this book can't cover every federal, state, or local law that will apply to your situation. The purpose of this chapter is simply to make you aware of some of the restrictions you might come under as well as some of the types of taxes you might be responsible for paying.

I recommend that you seek competent legal and financial advice and keep good records. Attorney and CPA fees should be factored in to the cost of opening and running your business. It is the best money you will ever spend. Do your homework by first researching at the library or on the Internet and by calling the offices of regulatory agencies with any questions you may have. It can be time-consuming and costly to set up one business entity only to find it is not the right type for you.

Sole Proprietorship

This is the fastest, easiest, and cheapest business entity to set up. In most cases, you don't even need a business name. You are the sole owner and you take all the responsibility for paying the bills and taxes, and you have full legal liability for your business. In most cases, sole proprietors file a Schedule C along with their personal income-tax returns.

Partnership

Partnerships are similar to sole proprietorships except there are two or more people who share the work and the financial and legal responsibility of the company. Filling out tax returns for a partnership is more complicated. When entering into a partnership, it is best to have an agreement in writing about how to handle business and personal situations that might arise, such as the death of a partner, taking in new partners, or how to handle the assets if one partner wants out.

Remember that a partnership is almost like a marriage. No matter how long you have been friends and how well you get along, at some point in time, you'll disagree on something. Ending a partnership can be like going through a divorce, so it's best to address how different situations are to be handled before they come up.

Corporation

There are C-Corporations and S-Corporations. These can be complicated and expensive to start and to keep records for. Each type is taxed differently. Often people incorporate for tax advantages and to ensure that they are not personally responsible for the liabilities of the corporation. A CPA can best advise you on the pros and cons of incorporating and all the forms that need to be completed.

Limited Liability Company (LLC)

The LLC gives you protection from personal liability and gives you the tax advantages of a sole proprietorship or partnership. You must file with the appropriate state office. Depending on where you live, you may need to pay franchise or corporation fees or some other fees to the state.

SELF-EMPLOYMENT TAXES

Be aware that self-employed people do not have income and social security taxes withheld from their income as do people who earn a regular paycheck from an employer. You'll need to pay self-employment taxes quarterly or yearly, depending on your income level. Throughout the year, you should consider setting aside part of your income for the payment of these taxes. Otherwise, it could be difficult to come up with the money when the taxes are due.

CHAPTER 4

Working at Home

*I*t is natural for "civilian" quiltmakers to compare your quilting service to the joy they get from choosing fabric, cutting it up into pieces, and stitching it into a beautiful quilt top. However, all too often the joy we experience in making and quilting our own quilts is not fully transferred when we begin quilting for others. Now it's business. In this chapter, we'll look at some of the realities of being self-employed in your home and running a quilting service.

Working in Solitude

If you need to interact with coworkers around you each day, this is probably not the business for you. Unless you have a computerized system or an employee, to make money in machine quilting you must use your hands and concentrate on your work. It is much different than going to an office each day and meeting and talking with coworkers. If you need human interaction, schedule activities in your week so you won't go nuts from being alone. If you prefer solitude in heavy doses, you should be fine.

Child Care

One possible reason you've decided to start a business in your home is to spend more time with your children. Working at home while taking care of children is a tremendous juggling act. Most children can be taught that you need uninterrupted time for business activities, but their ages will determine how much of that time you can actually spend on your business. Having small children in your house means numerous interruptions, which leads to less efficient use of your time. If you have small children at home, consider some sort of child-care arrangement. Have someone else watch your children while you work uninterrupted for a few hours, and use this time to quilt. It can be a great opportunity for your children to spend time with grandparents, aunts, uncles, or cousins. Some churches and community organizations have mother's day–out programs a few days a week. These sessions are usually inexpensive and give your preschool children a chance to learn and play with children their own age.

If your children are of school age, you'll have a chance to quilt most of the day without interruption. The younger my children were, the less I got accomplished when they were home. Also, each day between 4 P.M. and 7 P.M. is a very hectic time. Your children and spouse come home and need to wind down a little, have a snack, or play. It's time to prepare dinner, eat, and clean up. Homework needs to be done. If you are raising children now or have already raised yours, you know the drill! If this is the case in your home, save yourself a lot of frustration and don't attempt to schedule business activities during this prime family time. As your children grow older and take on more responsibility, you'll find life less hectic.

Household Chores

Who will do the household chores and when? Delegate chores to each family member and schedule when they are to be done. If you are doing the cleaning and cooking yourself, schedule those activities in your workweek. (Remember the calendar exercise on page 8?)

You may prefer to do all the chores in one day or to schedule a different chore for each day. Schedule a chore such as laundry at a time that allows for frequent interruptions. Conducting client appointments, doing laundry, and piecing a quilt each involves frequent stopping points. Combine all three of these tasks on one day to really get a lot done. You might also consider "power cooking," where you prepare several meals in one day.

Hiring people to do the work for you is another option. If you hire a cleaning person who can do the job better and faster, the time you don't spend cleaning the house can be used to quilt. If you make more than enough money from the quilting to pay for the cleaning person, you are ahead of the game.

Working with Another Person

I often wish I had an extra pair of hands to help with loading a quilt onto the machine, basting, answering the phone, or meeting clients. If you have a spouse, friend, or relative who is interested in your business, they could be a wonderful help to you. If that friend or relative is a quilter, you could offer to quilt for them in exchange for their helping out occasionally.

If you decide to hire someone to work for you, check the IRS rules and regulations regarding employees. You could find yourself liable for half of their social security taxes or other withholdings. If your friend stitches bindings in her home using her own equipment and supplies, the IRS considers her an independent contractor, responsible for her own taxes. If you pay her $600 or more in a year, you are required to file IRS Form 1099 for the amount you paid to her. With this arrangement, your friend is able to make a little extra money for herself and you are able to offer your clients binding services without cutting into your quilting time.

GETTING AND STAYING MOTIVATED

For me, the way to stay motivated is to have a strict routine with lots of variety. If I get out of my routine, I get nothing done. Other, more free-spirited people shun routines and are able to get their work done without one. Here are some other ways to stay on track.

- Recharge yourself during the day by including breaks in your routine. Take the dog for a walk; you'll both feel better.
- Give yourself little rewards, such as watching your favorite show or reading a chapter of a good book.
- To keep stress levels down, get enough sleep and exercise, and drink plenty of water.
- Sit down for lunch or dinner. Don't stand in front of the refrigerator and shovel it in. If you have a stand-up quilting system, you're already spending enough time on your feet.
- For inspiration, browse through a quilting book or magazine.

Working around Your Spouse

Some of us have spouses who are very supportive and encouraging of what we do, but who have no desire to pitch in and help. Before starting your business, talk with your spouse about the time and effort involved in running your business. Discuss how he or she can help you in the business and with household and personal chores. Have a clear understanding of who is responsible for what. In many cases, if you show your spouse your business plan, calendar, and expected income, you'll be taken seriously—this is not some little thing you're doing to pass the time. Hopefully, your spouse will begin to understand when he or she sees the extra income.

Physical Concerns

Working all day at a stand-up quilting machine can be demanding on your feet, ankles, legs, back, neck, and shoulders as well as other parts of your body. Sitting to quilt can be demanding on your back, neck, arms, and shoulders. If your body allows you to stand or sit for only short periods of time, include this factor in your calendar when scheduling quilting time.

If you use a wheelchair, make sure you can comfortably operate your quilting or sewing machine while in your chair. It is not impossible to quilt, but it may take a little extra time, so consider that as well.

It is important to work in a way that doesn't stress or injure your body. Prevention is the best medicine. Here are my tips for treating your body right.

- Always stand or sit up straight with good posture. Ladies might try a posture or sports bra with lots of support for the back.
- Relax your fingers, hands, wrists, arms, and shoulders while you are quilting. We tend to tense up, especially when our machine is new or we are concentrating on the quilting. Relax and remember to breathe.
- Keep your wrist straight, not bent. If this is difficult to do, purchase a wrist brace that holds your wrist straight. Measure your wrist for proper sizing. Keep your elbows bent at a 90° angle.

◆ If you stand on a hard floor, get a mat or other surface made for standing. It should cover the length of the machine on both sides.

◆ If you sit at a machine, your chair should be sturdy, supportive, and comfortable. Again, your elbows should be bent 90° while you quilt.

◆ Never quilt for more than two hours at a time. Quilt for an hour or so; then stop and put your feet up for 10 minutes before going back to quilting. After your break, try some stretching exercises to loosen your muscles, and drink a glass of water. You will be relaxed and ready for the next round of quilting.

◆ Never quilt in your bare feet. You need comfortable shoes with good support. No flip-flops here. Pins and needles always seem to land on the floor out of sight until you walk around in your bare feet. Clients might bring in quilt tops with rusty pins that could fall out, so keep your tetanus shots up to date, too.

◆ If you have arthritis or stiffness in your hands, consider adding options to your machine, such as the needle up/down function for quilting and sewing machines or a stitch regulator for quilting machines. These features reduce the repetitive finger and wrist motions.

KEEPING BUSINESS AND PERSONAL LIFE SEPARATE

With a home business, personal and professional lines are blurred. You live in your workplace and work in your home. If you have trouble separating your work life and home life, here are some suggestions.

◆ When the phone rings, you might want to take calls from your spouse or your children's school. Other calls, including business calls, can wait until your scheduled time to return calls. This minimizes the number of interruptions. Use an answering machine and caller ID to screen your calls.

◆ On your brochures, advertisements, and business cards, print your business hours and leave off your address. When clients call you outside of your business hours, let the machine answer the call; return the call when you "open" the next business day. Give out your address and directions after the client has made an appointment.

◆ Check your schedule every day and work only during the designated hours. Just as you would get up from your desk and leave the office at 5 P.M., you should stop working at the end of your day.

◆ If you enjoy quilting, schedule time to be with quilting friends and time to quilt for yourself. Don't lose your beloved hobby to your business.

CHAPTER 5

Setting Prices

Before opening the doors to your business, you need to determine your charges. What you charge for your services should be fair to you and your client. If you set your rates too low, you might feel you are giving away your services and not making the most money you can. While we touched on the topic of pricing in chapter 1, in this chapter we'll look more closely at how to charge for your services and how to give you the tools you need for setting fees.

The two most common ways to charge for quilting are by the hour and by the size of the quilt. My personal preference is to charge by quilt size because I like to give my clients a firm price when they drop off their quilts. If I charged by the hour, I would need to give accurate estimates of the cost and then keep

track of every minute I work on each project. I find it less confusing to the client and easier for me to have simple pricing. I quote one price that includes quilting, loading, basting, and paperwork. What works best for me is to have one price for allover designs and a different price for custom work.

Whether you charge by the hour or by the quilt size, you need to know how long it takes to complete certain tasks. This is not only good for scheduling purposes but it also enables you to set fair prices. Use an inexpensive stopwatch or timer to time yourself doing different tasks, and record those times in a timing chart. Stop the watch if you are called away from your quilting, and start it up again when you return. This is another reason I don't like charging by the hour. It means you are tied to the stopwatch each time you work. In the sections that follow, I'll explain which activities and tasks to time and how to use that data to determine a cost per surface area.

Timing Chart

As you time yourself completing various activities, record your times in a timing chart, filling it out over the course of a few weeks. Once you have a few weeks worth of data, use it to determine prices for those services. The chart below is what high-volume professional quilters using a stand-up machine might use. It consists of five columns with the following headings:

Quilt. Identify this quilt somehow, such as "Nine Patch" or "Log Cabin."

Size. Record the width and length in inches.

Loading time. Write down the time it took you to load the quilt.

Quilting time. Keep track of the time it took you to quilt the entire quilt.

Other time or technique. Use this column to record other tasks or specialty tasks, such as outline quilting, trapunto, or marking a grid.

Customize your chart to include activities you do routinely when quilting. If you sit at your machine to quilt, you might replace the "Loading Time" column with "Basting Time" or "Marking Time."

Loading or basting. Start the timer as you begin loading the machine or basting the top and stop when the quilt is ready to be quilted. Include the time it takes to oil and clean the machine, wind the bobbins, thread needles, tape down the backing, and any other prep work. These are all things that need to be done for each quilt and should be considered as part of the loading or basting process.

Marking and pattern prep. Time how long it takes to mark either the entire quilt or several blocks in a quilt. You might also want to include a column for removing markings later.

Allover quilting. Write down the name of the pattern you are quilting. Some heavily quilted designs can take as much as twice the time as designs with

TIMING CHART				
Quilt	Size	Loading Time	Quilting Time	Other Time / Technique
Butterflies Allover	68" x 68"	52 minutes	3 hours	
Lace Allover	85" x 105"	90 minutes	6 hours	

less quilting, so you might want to charge more for these. It is not necessary to time the quilting of the entire quilt. Instead, time the quilting of about four or five rows and then measure the length and width of the area you quilted. Multiply the two numbers to calculate the square inches of that area.

As you become familiar with each pattern, you'll find that a certain speed or stitch length works better for that particular pattern. On the pattern itself, write down the motor-speed setting or the stitch length that worked best for you. Next time you use that pattern, set the motor speed or stitch length written on the pattern.

Custom quilting. Learning the different quilting techniques required for custom machine quilting is slow-going at first, but the more you practice them, the better you get. Time and record each of these quilting techniques separately, including quilting motifs in blocks, quilting set-in borders, doing freehand or meander quilting, and turning the quilt. If you are stitching in the ditch, time and record how long it takes to do several blocks. Make a note of how much stitching in the ditch was involved—a little or a lot.

Unloading the quilt. Once the quilting is finished, you need to clip threads and prepare the quilt for customer pickup. Whatever your procedure is, record the time it takes to do it. Include in this total the time it takes to fold and bag the quilt for pickup as well as the time it takes to prepare the invoice and call the client.

Other activities. You might offer other services or activities that you wish to time and record separately, such as attaching binding, sewing seams, preparing patterns, talking to clients, or handling paperwork. Prepare and complete your timing chart to fit your needs.

EFFICIENT QUILTING

As you establish routines for various tasks—such as loading, basting, or marking a quilt—look for ways to save time. If you find yourself going from one side of the table to the other, repeating certain tasks, or starting and stopping often, there is probably a more efficient method. Mentally rehearse or write down the steps required to complete a task and see where you can combine or omit some steps. Shaving off even a few minutes of time has a positive effect on your bottom line.

For example, I routinely took 45 minutes or more to load a quilt on my long-arm machine because I would go from one side to the other, doing first one task on one side and then on the other side. Then I'd repeat the process for the next task. When I combined all the tasks on one side before moving to the other side to repeat them (with some other minor changes), I could load any size quilt in 25 minutes or less. The 20 minutes saved may sound insignificant, but when you multiply that by three quilts per week, you have an extra hour each week for other things.

Surface Area of a Quilt

A square yard is 36" by 36", so 1 square yard = 36" x 36" = 1296 square inches. Usually a quilt top is measured in inches, so if you measure the width of the quilt by the length of the quilt in inches and then multiply these numbers, you get the square inches of the quilt top. This represents the surface area of the quilt in square inches. Example: a quilt that measures 75" x 95" is 7125 square inches (75 x 95 = 7125).

If you charge by the square inch, multiply the price per square inch by this number to determine the quilting price. With a charge of $0.03 per square inch, the charge for this quilt is $213.75 (7125 x 0.03 = 213.75).

If you charge by the square foot or the square yard, you need to convert the square inches to square feet or square yards. For square feet, divide the square inches by 144. Example: 7125 ÷ 144 = 49.48 square feet. If you charge $4.25 per square foot, the charge for this quilt is $210.29 (49.48 x 4.25 = 210.29).

For square yards, divide the square inches by 1296. Example: 7125 ÷ 1296 = 5.5 square yards. If you charge $38 per square yard, the charge for this quilt is $209. (5.5 x 38 = 209).

Quiltmakers are familiar with associating a dollar amount with a yard of fabric, and a square yard is slightly smaller than the surface of one yard of fabric. Charging by the square yard makes the numbers easier to comprehend—7125 square inches versus 5½ square yards; $0.03 versus $38.

Recording Data

After you have timed yourself doing various activities, you can calculate how long it takes you to complete those activities based on the surface area. Instead of saying that it takes you four hours to do an allover design on a twin-size quilt, you will know how long it takes you to do an allover design over a specific surface area of any quilt. This information helps you in two ways. First, you are able to give the client estimates based on the actual quilt size instead of an estimated size. After all, one person's idea of a twin-size quilt could be what another person calls a full-size quilt. Second, when scheduling time to complete a quilt, you have a good estimate of the time it will take to complete that quilt. For example, I know from my timing chart that allover quilting takes me one hour per square yard while custom quilting takes me one to two hours per square yard.

Let's look at how to use the information from your timing chart to determine how long it takes to complete a certain task and then how to set your prices based on that time. The process includes:

◆ Combining similar data
◆ Finding the average time of certain activities
◆ Finding the quilting time per surface area
◆ Calculating a price for each service

COMBINING SIMILAR DATA

The first step is to combine the similar data and use that for your calculations. For example, combine all the data for marking quilts, all the data for stipple quilting, all the data for allover quilting, and all the data for stitching patterns in blocks. Remember, we are trying to get estimates here, so keep it simple. You can always do more calculations later if you like. If you want to separate your allover quilting into two categories (simple and complex), then do that as well. The chart below shows the combined data for allover quilting designs and includes the loading times for those quilts. We then use this data to determine how long it takes to quilt an allover design.

FINDING AVERAGE TIME PER TASK

From the chart, we can calculate the average time it takes to load a quilt. Add together all the loading times and divide by the number of entries: 52 + 90 + 70 + 45 = 257 minutes. Divide the total by the number of entries: 257 minutes ÷ 4 = 64.25 minutes. The average loading time for these four quilts is just over one hour. To keep things simple, just call it an hour. Calculate average times for basting and marking in the same way.

TIME DATA			
Allover Quilting Design	Quilt Size	Loading Time	Quilting Time
Butterfly	68" x 68"	52 minutes	3 hours
Lace	85" x 105"	90 minutes	6 hours
Meandering	77" x 94"	70 minutes	5 hours
Butterfly	45" x 60"	45 minutes	2 hours

DETERMINING QUILTING TIME PER SURFACE AREA

I like to calculate my fees based on square yards, so my examples are based on square yards. I've also included the data in square inches and square feet for your convenience.

To determine the average quilting time per square yard, first convert the size of the quilt from inches to square yards. To do this, multiply the length of the quilt by the width of the quilt and divide by 1296 (the number of square inches in a square yard). Note: Divide the total by 144 if you are using square feet.

68" x 68" = 4624 square inches
4624 ÷ 1296 = 3.57 square yards
4624 ÷ 144 = 32.11 square feet

The table below shows the same quilt sizes used in the previous table converted to square inches, square feet, and square yards.

CONVERSION TABLE				
Allover Quilting Design	Quilt Size	Square Inches	Square Feet	Square Yards
Butterfly	68" x 68"	4624	32.11	3.57
Lace	85" x 105"	8925	62.00	6.89
Meandering	77" x 94"	7238	50.26	5.58
Butterfly	45" x 60"	2700	18.75	2.08

To calculate the quilting time per square yard for each entry, divide the quilting time by the square yards. For instance, the allover butterfly design took three hours and is 3.57 square yards: $3 \div 3.57 = .84$ hours per square yard. The time per surface area for each example quilt is calculated for you below.

What do these numbers tell you so far? The highest number is .96 hours per square yard and the lowest number is .84 hours per square yard. All times are just under one hour per square yard, so you can conclude that all the patterns you quilted in this sample took about one hour per square yard to quilt. If your numbers come out to just over an hour, I would round up to 1¼ hours to add a factor of safety.

When you combine all of the similar data, the numbers should be very similar to one another. If you have numbers that vary greatly, you might want to calculate an average for those numbers. Add the numbers together and divide by 4. Example: $.84 + .87 + .90 + .96 = 3.57 \div 4 = .89$ hours per square yard. Another way to deal with the situation if your results are not all similar is to see which of the numbers is different. Perhaps the pattern is more complicated and should go in a different category than "allover quilting."

Now you know that when you quilt an allover design, it will take you about one hour per square yard. Remember, this is just quilting time and does not include loading the quilt or doing the paperwork.

TIME PER SQUARE YARD			
Allover Quilting Design	Quilting Time	Square Yard	Time per Square Yard
Butterfly	3 hours	3.57	.84 hours
Lace	6 hours	6.89	.87 hours
Meandering	5 hours	5.58	.90 hours
Butterfly	2 hours	2.08	.96 hours

CALCULATING PRICES

Armed with the calculations made above, you can decide how you want to set your prices, based on either a price per hour or a price per surface area.

Price per hour. Now that you know how long it takes for the quilting, you can determine the price to charge if you wish to charge by the hour. Say you charge $25 per hour and the quilt is 5.4 square yards. You know it takes one hour per square yard, so the quilting charge is calculated as: $25 per hour x 5.4 (square yards x 1 hour per square yard) = $135.

Remember, this is the price for quilting time only. For a complete cost estimate for your client, you must include loading, marking, and paperwork time if applicable. If it takes you an additional two hours for these activities and your charge is $25 per hour, add this to the quilting charge: $25 per hour x 2 hours = $50. The total charge would be: $135 + $50 = $185.

Price per surface area. To charge by surface area, use the following formula: time to load a quilt plus an hour per square yard to quilt an allover design, plus an hour for paperwork and appointments: 1 hour + 5.4 hours + 1 hour = 7.4 hours.

If you want to make $25 per hour in your business, the charge for this quilt is: 7.4 hours x $25 per hour = $185. To determine the rate to charge to get this amount, divide by the number of square yards. In this example: $185 ÷ 5.4 square yards = $34.26 per square yard. If you charge $34.26 per square yard for allover quilting, you will make approximately $25 per hour for each quilt. I would round up this result to $35 per square yard to make calculations easier.

To find out the rate to charge for custom quilting, go through the same steps as above. Remember to include the loading and paperwork time.

With the price-per-surface-area method, you don't need to be concerned with keeping track of

time for each task after you set up your initial prices. Periodically, you'll want to gather new data to see if you've become more efficient in your work or to adjust your prices.

Batting

If you choose to offer batting to your clients, it is more economical if you purchase large rolls at wholesale cost. I charge for batting by the inch and calculate the cost to the client as described below.

YOUR COST

Take the cost of the batting and add all the other charges, such as shipping and handling. If a 30-yard roll of batting costs $90 plus $12 shipping, then the cost per inch would be: ($90 + $12) ÷ 30 yards ÷ 36" = 9 cents per inch. Note that this is a linear inch, not square inches.

MARKUP ON RETAIL PRICE

You know the batting costs you 9 cents per inch. Now you need to mark up that cost to get the retail price to charge your client. Usually the markup from wholesale to retail is double; however, I found that this price was way undercutting my local quilt shops. I use a markup of 3.5 times the cost, which gives a retail price just under what quilt shops charge: 9 cents x 3.5 = 31.5 cents per inch (which I'd round up to 32 cents per inch).

COST TO CLIENT

Try to waste as little batting as possible, but be sure you don't run out of it at the end of the quilt. I like to have an extra 10" of batting in the length. For the width, you can get away with less because when the quilt is loaded on the frame, you can see if the batting is wide enough. Rolls of batting come in various widths and the most common sizes for professional quilters are 96" and 108".

The illustration below shows the most efficient way to cut batting for a 75" x 86" quilt top. The 96" width of the batting can accommodate the longest side of the quilt with only a few inches of waste batting on the sides. Notice that if you place the quilt lengthwise on the batting, you waste much more batting.

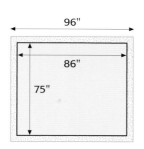

Efficient Use of Batting

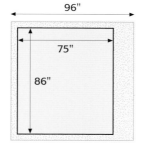

Inefficient Use of Batting

Using the orientation shown above left and adding 10" to the length, the batting charge to the client is calculated as follows: (75" + 10") x 32 cents per inch = $27.20. If you followed the other orientation, shown above right, you'd need to charge (86" + 10") x 32 cents = $30.72.

Price Increases

When preparing a price list of your services and products or when preparing a brochure, include the words "Prices subject to change without notice." Also include an effective date for your prices. You might want to include language that says the prices to be charged are the prices in effect at the time the quilt is delivered for service. This means that if you have a waiting list as long as a year and you decide to raise your prices in six months, whatever price is in effect at the time the client drops off the quilt is the price

that is charged. Some people hold on to price lists and brochures for several years. For your protection, be sure to prominently display these statements.

When you are ready to raise your prices, publish new brochures with the new prices and the effective date. Unless you have given firm prices or have signed a contract for work, begin charging the new prices on the effective date.

When should you raise your prices? Two situations justify price increases: when your costs increase and as your abilities improve. If you need justification of a higher price, you can point to your experience. If you have spent time and money taking classes that improve your quilting skills, you deserve a raise. If quilts you have quilted win awards, your services should become more valuable.

When my business was new, my prices were quite low and I raised them every four to six months for the first year and a half. I would keep new timing charts to make sure I was charging a fair price. Once I established a routine and gained more experience, I limited my price increases to once a year.

MINIMUM FEES

Whether you charge by time or surface area, undoubtedly the charge for quilting small quilts will add up to a small amount. However, you still need to make appointments, talk to the client, prepare the paperwork, etc. So, in order to be properly compensated for all of your time, consider implementing a minimum charge. At the very least, your minimum should be equivalent to two hours of your time. If you wish to make $25 per hour, set your minimum charge at $50.

CHAPTER 6

What Services Will You Offer?

When your business is new, offer the services that you know well, such as basic quilting techniques and binding. Add services or products as your skill and confidence levels increase. In this chapter we'll take a look at the variety of services you may eventually want to offer. Mastering the quilting techniques described here will require some kind of instruction, such as through classes, videotapes, CDs, or books—and of course, hands-on practice (see "Resources" page 75).

Quilting

Quilting is your bread and butter. Your quilting services can range from allover quilting only to free-motion quilting to custom-quilting techniques. After timing these services to see how long they take, you'll want to set prices for each type of service that you plan to offer.

ALLOVER QUILTING

Also known as pantograph quilting, panto, edge-to-edge quilting, or basic quilting, allover quilting is usually the first type of quilting learned on the stand-up quilting system. Many suppliers offer a variety of patterns, and most machine manufacturers include a set of patterns with the machine purchase.

Keep a catalog or flyers of pattern designs to show your clients what is available. Build up your stock of allover patterns by ordering them as your clients request them. You can usually order and receive a pattern in a few days, so waiting to order patterns until you need them shouldn't impact your schedule.

Allover quilting at a sit-down machine generally means free-motion quilting a repeating or free-form pattern over the entire quilt. Methods for pricing allover quilting are discussed in "Setting Prices" on page 35.

CUSTOM QUILTING

I consider anything that is not allover quilting to be custom quilting. As a professional quilter who offers custom quilting, you will find it is to your advantage to learn as many techniques as you can so you'll have a variety of design options for your clients.

As you progress in your profession through learning new techniques and gaining experience, it makes sense for you to charge higher rates for custom work than for basic services. However, custom quilting can become a time hog, and you could find that you are pricing many of your clients out of your league. To get paid what you are worth and still have a sufficient client base, find ways to complete each quilting task faster and better. Completing a task in a shorter amount of time and still charging the same rates is effectively giving yourself a raise. You'll make the same amount of money in less time.

As discussed in "Setting Prices," I prefer to charge the same fee for any type of custom-quilting

service. However, if you choose to set different fees for different services, that can work as well.

STIPPLE OR MEANDER QUILTING

Simple meander stitching is what many quiltmakers refer to as stippling. The stitching does not cross over itself and has a serpentine look. The size of the meander is determined by the distance between the stitching lines; it can be as small or as large as needed. For me, a small meander is less than ½" apart; medium meander about 1" apart; large meander is over 1". These are not rigid standards but merely guidelines for keeping the stipple size uniform. Choose and set your own guidelines, stitch samples of meandering in various sizes, and identify each size with a letter or number. Clients can choose the size they prefer by looking at the samples and you can refer to it as you stitch. The smaller the stipple, the longer it takes to fill an area, so consider charging a little bit more for the smaller stipple.

Various Sizes of Stipple Meandering

Patterned meander, also called free-form or freehand quilting, is meandering with a purpose. Here you can make up the design as you go or choose one design to repeat in different sizes and orientations. It is a quick way to complete a quilt or parts of a quilt, such as plain setting blocks or borders. This meandering can be compared to doodling designs on paper. In fact, it's best to audition designs using a pencil and paper before going to the quilting machine to stitch.

Many professional quilters develop their own designs to meander in a quilt. These designs are beautiful to look at, especially when they're stitched with decorative threads. Consider charging more for patterned meander than you do for simple meander.

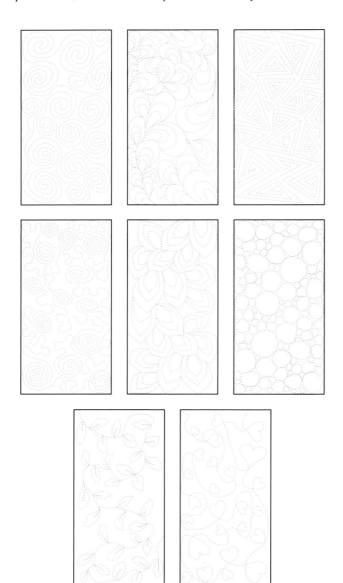

Examples of Patterned Meandering

PATTERN MOTIFS

These designs are stitched by using a laser light to follow a printed pattern placed on the table or a pattern marked on the quilt top. Because pattern motifs must be sized to fit, positioned, or marked on the quilt, they require more time to complete. Consider charging a little extra for this type of quilting. The additional cost could be included in an overall custom quilting charge or it could be an additional dollar or two per block. Stencils are often used to mark pattern motifs in blocks, borders, and sashes.

SET-IN BORDERS

When borders are stitched with a hand-guided machine from a printed pattern, in most cases it requires that the quilt be unloaded, turned, and reloaded to complete the design. This is a time-consuming task, so consider an extra charge, such as a set-in border, remounting, or turning fee.

STITCH IN THE DITCH

Most quiltmakers press seam allowances to one side as they piece their quilt tops. This creates a ditch on the side of the seam without the bulk of the seam allowances. Stitching in the ditch means to stitch just to the side of the seam line in the "ditch" created by the pressing. Because seams are never perfectly straight (fabric is flexible, after all), it takes time and skill to stitch neatly in the ditch using a stand-up machine; you should charge accordingly.

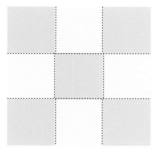

Quilting in the Ditch

OUTLINE QUILTING

Quilting ¼" from the seam line is called outline quilting. If you outline every patch, you are doing twice the work than if you had stitched in the ditch of those seams, and it requires a lot of starting and stopping. Custom quilting charges should apply.

Outline Quilting

ECHO QUILTING

Echo quilting is a nice way to fill in the background behind either patchwork or appliqué. Whether you're stitching around an appliqué or parallel to the patchwork seam lines, this is free-form stitching that again requires skill and practice.

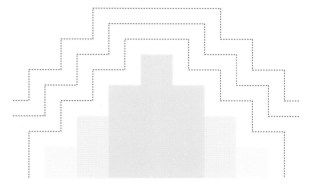

Echo Quilted Patchwork

Echo Quilted Appliqué

CONTINUOUS-CURVE QUILTING

With this fast method, you stitch through the intersections of the seams, using them as your guide. It is similar to outline quilting in that you are stitching a distance away from the seam. However, in order to quickly move from one patch to the next, you stitch through the intersection instead of having to turn a corner. If you plan your path correctly, you can quilt large areas without stopping.

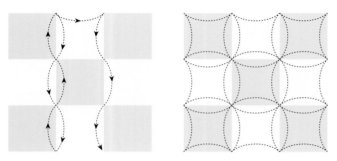

Continuous-Curve Quilting

TRAPUNTO

Trapunto, or stuffed work, is an easy yet time-consuming task. You should have a firm estimate of the time required to complete it before setting prices for this technique. Some trapunto techniques require the quilt top to be unloaded so that the trapunto batting can be trimmed away before completing the rest of the quilting. To reduce the likelihood of cutting a client's quilt top while cutting away the excess batting, some professional quilters require the client to trim the trapunto batting before the second loading. If you have a similar policy, let your client know before starting the quilt.

If you have mail-order clients, you may want to consider one of the following options for handling trapunto:

◆ Don't offer it for mail-order clients.
◆ Have the client release you from liability.
◆ Have the client pay for shipping the quilt top back and forth before the second loading.

GRID QUILTING

Grid quilting consists of parallel, straight lines. You can stitch them horizontally, vertically, or at an angle. Cross-hatching is when an area is stitched first in one direction, then again in the opposite direction. It is always a good idea to mark grids, whether you're quilting at a stand-up system or at a sit-down machine, to ensure that the spacing between the lines is uniform throughout. Some long-arm machine quilters are able to stitch grids without marking; however, it is easy for the grid to become distorted when you use this method.

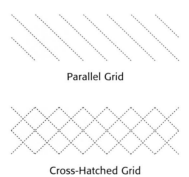

Parallel Grid

Cross-Hatched Grid

Basting

Many quiltmakers like to hand quilt all or most of their work, and you might think that these people will never be your clients. Consider offering basting services to your clients who hand quilt or machine quilt for themselves. Basting is a tedious and time-consuming task to do by hand, but on a long-arm machine you can baste a full-size quilt in about two hours. What quilter wouldn't appreciate the value of having someone else baste her quilt?

Binding

Offering binding services can be a good way to add extra income to your business. If you do not like to do bindings but have a neighbor or friend close by who sews, perhaps she wouldn't mind making a little extra money doing bindings for your clients. It is easier to manage if you are located near each other and have compatible schedules. Once the quilting is finished, hand it over to the binder. Keep a portion of the binding fee for yourself and pay the rest to the binder. Generally, you will take payment from the client and pay the binder separately so that your client doesn't have to write two checks. For IRS requirements regarding contract employees, see "Working with Another Person" on page 28.

Some of your clients may like to prepare the binding but not attach it. Others don't mind hand stitching it down after it's attached. Still others will give you a yard of fabric and want you to make, attach, and finish the binding. A convenient way to charge for binding services is to break down the steps involved in completing the task: preparing binding, attaching binding, and finishing binding by hand or by sewing machine.

PREPARING AND ATTACHING BINDING

Preparing the binding means cutting the strips, sewing them together end to end, and pressing them wrong sides together. For this, I charge 8 cents per inch. Attaching the binding means to sew it to the front of the quilt by machine. For this, I also charge 8 cents per inch. Time yourself doing these tasks and add them to your timing chart. I like to charge by the perimeter in inches for binding services. For example, a 75" x 95" quilt has a perimeter of 75 + 75 + 95 + 95 = 340 inches. If the client brings in this quilt and wants me to prepare (8 cents) and attach (8 cents) a binding that she will later hand stitch down, I calculate the charges as follows: $0.08 per inch + $0.08 per inch = $0.16 per inch; $0.16 per inch x 340 inches = $54.40.

HAND STITCHING

For this option, I double the cost of preparing and attaching. Generally, when I hand stitch a binding, I am not making my desired hourly wage. However, I think it is important that I offer binding services to my clients, and I justify a lower hourly rate to myself because I generally do the hand stitching while watching television. This is time that I didn't plan in my business anyway. Since I am not taking away from quilting time, I consider it earning extra money while relaxing! Others may disagree, so decide what is right for you.

If a client brings a prepared binding that she wants me to attach and hand stitch, I calculate the charges as follows: $.08 per inch (to attach) + $0.16 per inch (hand stitch) = $0.24 per inch; $0.24 per inch x 340 inches = $81.60.

Pressing Tops

Since it is best to avoid having the client bring a wrinkled quilt top, simply discuss pressing and other requirements such as those for the backing (see below) at the time you schedule the drop-off appointment. Often, new quiltmakers simply don't know what is best or what you require. I give them the option of having me press the top for a charge of $25 or more, depending on the size. Clients often ask if this pressing requirement applies to quilt tops and backings that arrive folded or boxed for shipping. The fold lines or small creases made by folding are not a problem if the fabric was pressed before folding. These folds and creases disappear once the fabric is loaded on the frame.

Backing

Backings should be at least 6" longer and wider than the quilt top. Measure the backing during the drop-off appointment and check to see if it is square. Often an out-of-square or insufficient backing can be avoided by mentioning it to the client when the appointment is scheduled. Occasionally, a client will bring a pieced backing and want you to center the quilt top with the pieced backing. This is something you can do if you quilt the layers after they have been basted. However, if you are using a quilting system that does not require basting, this is harder to do.

For hand-guided quilting in which the quilt is loaded on the frame without basting, it is easy to center in one direction but not always possible in the other direction. Centering in the horizontal direction can be done by measuring or by eye. Attempts to center in the vertical direction (between the

rollers) means you might risk running out of backing fabric when you reach the bottom of the quilt.

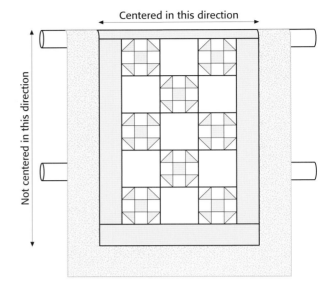

If the layers were laid out flat and hand- or pin-basted, the backing could be centered for quilting at a sit-down machine. However, stand-up quilting should not be done on a pre-basted quilt because of the possibility of puckers.

When you load the quilt on the frame, you can see that the width is properly centered; the width is not the problem. In order to center the length of the quilt, you need to first determine how far from the top edge of the backing the edge of the quilt top must be. Then you need to measure that distance from the top of the backing to place the quilt top. The top can shift slightly during quilting, causing the backing to become off-centered. If the backing is not quite large enough to handle this shifting, you run the risk of running out of backing fabric by the time you reach the end of the quilt. In cases where the client wants a centered backing, I tell them that I can get one direction centered but I cannot guarantee that the other direction will be exactly centered.

Often clients bring yardage for the backing and want you to piece it for them. If you offer this service, you should consider charging per seam to stitch and press. Usually there are no more than two seams in the backing.

If you are quilting at a sit-down machine, it is not as important that the backing be perfectly square. However, for stand-up quilting systems, the backing is pinned between the take-up roller and the backing roller, so it is important that the backing be square so the layers lie flat between the rollers. Squaring up a backing can take some time, so you should charge for this service. Measure the backing while the client is still there and check to see if it might need to be squared. For tips on squaring up the backing, see *Long-Arm Machine Quilting* (Martingale & Company, 2002).

Edge Basting

As you complete the quilting it is a good idea to baste along the outer edges of the quilt. Not only does it stabilize the quilt, but it also makes applying binding easier. If you routinely baste the edges, the time involved should be included as regular quilting time in your timing chart. If it is, you are being paid for this in your normal quilting fee and there is no need to add the cost.

Edge Trimming

After completing all quilting, many professional quilters like to trim the backing and batting even with the quilt top. However, your client may wish to have extra batting and backing for their bindings. Before trimming, be sure to consult your client for her or his preference regarding trimming. If trimming is okay, I prefer to trim about 1" away from the quilt top so there is extra room to square up the edges later.

Quilt Labels

If you like to prepare quilt labels, such as with an embroidery machine, you might consider offering to make and attach custom quilt labels for your clients, too. Prepare samples of whatever method you use and have them ready to display when the client drops off the quilt. Your charge for the label should include both the time it takes to make the label and to attach it.

CHAPTER 7

Marketing

Two of the most important considerations in marketing your business are advertising in the right places and advertising consistently. Target your advertising to prospective clients by looking for places that attract quilters, such as quilting magazines and quilt guilds.

Be consistent with your advertising. Prospective clients who see your ad one month may not require your services for another three or four months. If your advertising is not published each month, you might lose their business.

Quilt Shops

Quilt shops are the best places to get business. Call the owner of your local quilt shop and introduce yourself. Ask if you can set up an appointment to come in and show samples of your work. Take your best sample of quilting along with your business cards and brochures. Not all quilt-shop relationships work the same way. You can be totally independent of the shop or you can have an agreement where the shop has all the contact with the client. Let's look at a few possibilities.

INDEPENDENT SERVICE

To be completely independent from the quilt shop means that the shop refers its customers to you for quilting. You set your prices and the quilt shop does not get a percentage of your work. In most cases, this is the ideal situation. The quilt-shop owner benefits because many customers will purchase fabric and supplies for their next project after they've handed over a quilt top to be quilted.

Ask the owner if you can meet clients at the shop. This can have several advantages for both you and the owner. For you, you don't have clients come to your home. You can schedule the appointments closer to each other and accomplish more things in a shorter amount of time. The shop owner benefits because you are bringing customers into the shop. While they are there, chances are clients will shop around and spend a little money. My problem is keeping my checkbook closed when I go to meet customers at the shop!

You should be aware that if a shop refers their customers to you, you have a responsibility to conduct yourself in a businesslike manner. If your work is not up to par or if you do not treat your clients properly, the quilt shop will hear about it and you will be taken off the referral list. Even though you are independent of the quilt shop, you have the obligation to present yourself in a manner that reflects well on the shop and its owner.

PERCENTAGE TO SHOP OWNER

This relationship means that the quilt shop owner refers clients to you and allows you to use shop space for meeting with clients or agrees to take in quilts for you in exchange for a percentage of your profit. If you meet clients at the quilt shop, most of them will make it a dual-purpose trip—drop off their quilts and do a little shopping while they're there. If you pay a percentage to the quilt shop, try to negotiate a very small one or perhaps offer to quilt one class sample per month in lieu of a percentage. Shop owners are business people, too, and fair agreements are good for both of you.

SHOP TAKES IN QUILTS

In this arrangement, the shop takes in the quilts from its customers and hands them over to you for quilting. The customer and shop owner decide how to quilt the top; you don't usually have a relationship with the client.

This arrangement is fine if you don't want creative control over your work or if you decide to limit your quilting to certain patterns or techniques. Some professional quilters prefer this arrangement. They don't have clients calling and coming to their home, so they can work with fewer interruptions.

HAVING YOUR STUDIO IN THE SHOP

One way to solve the problem of limited space for a studio or for meeting clients is to have your studio located in a quilt shop. You pay rent to the shop owner for your space. Shop customers see you, your machine, and your work. In short, it's an ideal way to get clients. In this situation, you are helping the shop owner to pay some of the rent, and your clients come into the shop so you don't have to take up space in your home for your business.

On the down side, you will have numerous interruptions because the shop customers come in all day long and you must stop and talk with them even if they are not the least bit interested in leaving a quilt with you. They are curious about your services and want to see your work. They ask questions about your machine. Try to have the machine located in a back room or in a room behind a glass partition where you can quilt without interruption but allow customers to see you work.

Before you choose to have your machine set up in a quilt shop, you should consider whether or not you'd like to be working after hours. If you do not have access to your machine at all times, you are not able to quilt whenever you want to, which could limit your income potential. On the other hand, if access isn't a problem, you could work when the shop is closed. But do you really want to be alone in a shop at night and after the other businesses in the area are closed?

Referrals and Fees

Some quilt shops will ask for a referral fee to keep you on their referral list. If this price is not outrageous and you regularly get clients from the shop, then the fee is probably worth it. Consider the cost versus your benefits.

Often, you can have an agreement with another professional quilter where you each can refer clients to the other. This sort of reciprocating arrangement with another quilter can be helpful for times when one or the other of you is booked or if one does different types of quilting than the other. In short, it can be beneficial to both parties.

Business Cards

Keep a good supply of business cards on hand and with you at all times. Give one to each person who asks about your business and give one to each client who drops off a quilt. That way, your clients will have your information readily available and may even pass your card on to a friend.

The information you include on your cards should be minimal. Your business name, phone number, e-mail address, and Web site address are the most important things to include. You might also want to briefly describe your services. If you work from home, you may not want to include your address on your cards. Not everyone knows that you work out of your home and you might have people just drop by. Put "Appointment Only" and your business hours instead of your address. Give clients your address and directions only after they have made an appointment.

If you have a computer and printer, you can purchase card-stock paper and print your own cards. This is a good option if you want to change your cards at certain times. If you prefer not to print your own cards, you can order business cards from a local printer or office-supply store. You may have to order a minimum of 1,000 cards at a time to get a good price. It will take you a long time to use 1,000 cards, and if you have any information changes, such as a phone number or area code, you'll need to correct the cards by hand or recycle them after your new ones have arrived.

Brochures

Brochures may be the first impression a client has of your business. The style and appearance of the brochure reflect on you. The brochure does not have to be fancy or printed on glossy paper, but keep it neat, easy to read, and full of useful information. Your brochure should include your contact information, your services and prices, and your policies. In addition to informing prospective clients, the brochure can save you time by weeding out people who decide not to use your services. If you have just a phone number on a card, you'll get lots of curious people calling. With your services, prices, and policies clearly placed in your brochure, you'll prevent some of the unproductive calls.

Most word-processing software has a design template for brochures. You can fold 8½" x 11" paper into three sections, keeping one area set up for mailing addresses in case you want to mail your brochure. If you would rather use that space for information, you can always mail brochures in envelopes. Below are some of the important things you'll want to include in your brochure.

Prices. List the prices for all your services and products. If you have a complicated way of determining prices, you should either list an example of how to make the calculation or have a range of approximate prices for that particular service. Don't waste valuable brochure space with unclear or confusing information.

If you have many separate prices that are added on to your custom quilting charge or some other service, you might want to leave all of those charges off your brochure and mention that "custom prices start at . . ." or some other information that indicates possible higher prices. Display the effective date of your prices prominently and state that they are subject to change without notice.

Policies. If you want the batting and backing to measure 6" larger than the quilt top, list that in your brochure. Other important policies, such as pressing the quilt top and backing, should be listed on the brochure as well. Instead of writing a legal document, list the policies that the client should be aware of before they bring their quilt. If you have other policies, you can discuss them with the client over the phone or at the drop-off appointment.

Services and products. List the services and products you offer, such as custom quilt labels, binding services, and batting. Show sample pattern designs if you have the space. Most pattern designers will let you copy a small sample of their patterns for use in your brochure, but be sure to check the copyright notice when you purchase patterns.

Contact information. Your contact information should include your business name, your name, telephone and fax numbers, e-mail address, Web site address, and business hours. If you have a commercial location, list your address as well.

Local Marketing

Guild newsletters are an excellent place to have a consistent presence. Usually you can purchase a business-card ad for $60 to $100 per year. Provide the editor with a clean, clear copy of your ad. Check other guilds in the area and advertise in several of them.

A booth at a local quilt show can also be a good place to advertise your service and give prospective clients a chance to meet you and see samples of your work. All that is needed for the booth are a few tables, quilt displays, cards, brochures, and any other advertising trinkets to give away. If you are a guild member, enter several quilts that you have quilted. Ask some of your clients to enter their quilts or to let you enter them. Make sure the entry application and show identification card reflect your name as the quilter.

All quilt guilds have a show-and-share portion of their meetings. Ask clients if you can show their quilts during this time and show your own quilts as well. Give a little sentence or two to describe the type of quilting that you did and why you chose it.

That draws attention directly to the quilting. Often, if I have quilts ready to return to clients who I know are attending a guild meeting, I call and ask if they would like me to bring the quilt to the meeting (or pick one up at the meeting). This saves time for me and for them because they don't have to make an appointment to come to me. The most quilts I ever returned at a guild meeting was six for five different people. At 30 minutes each for return appointments, I saved myself 2½ hours of appointment time since I was going to the meeting anyway.

Arrange to meet the client before the meeting starts so you don't disrupt the proceedings. Usually they want to see the quilt as soon as they spot you, so the quilt is quickly unfolded and admired. I don't have to tell you how fast you can gather a crowd around a new quilt at a quilt-guild meeting! It's great advertising and it's free. At show-and-share, most of them proudly display their creation and usually mention your name as the quilter. Don't be upset if someone does not mention your name even if you are right there. I have had clients come and apologize for forgetting to mention my name because they were so nervous presenting in front of a group that they couldn't think straight.

Internet

If possible, maintain a Web page—it's a good place to display photos of your work and give out information. Most Internet service providers offer a free, limited-use home page with your account. Some providers limit the file size and others limit you to just text—no pictures. Included in these accounts are the tools necessary to create and publish your Web page. Check with your provider to see what is available to you.

Another option is to use a picture-hosting Web site. These Internet businesses offer a spot to display picture albums for free or for a small fee. If you have a digital camera or printed photos and a scanner, you can upload pictures to the Internet using your computer. Include the Web site or a picture-site address on your business cards and brochures.

Magazines

Classified ads in magazines are another good place to advertise, especially if you want to develop mail-order business. These ads reach people all over the country and the world. Some of these readers don't have professional quilters in their area and don't mind shipping their quilts.

Keep the information in the ad short and to the point. Ads are charged by the word and if you want bold or shaded words, they cost extra. Magazines with high circulation have higher ad prices. Try sample ads in a few magazines and see what kind of response you get. Ask people how they heard about your services and keep track of which ads are working; discontinue those that aren't drawing clients for you.

Donations

Another way to get exposure for your business is to donate items or your services. Be sure you have some control over the item or service that you donate. If you are donating an entire quilt, set some minimums on the amount of money that the charity collects for the item. You don't want to donate a twin-size quilt and learn that it only takes in $25 for the charity. Choose the items and the charity carefully.

Donating to your quilt guild can give you good advertising and can benefit the guild at the same time. If you sell packaged batting and your guild has a mini raffle or drawing at each meeting, donate a batting for the raffle. Ask them to mention your name when the raffle is announced.

Another donation you can give to your guild auction is your quilting service. Make up a printed certificate to be given to the winner. (You can find blank certificates at office-supply stores or you can print customized certificates from your computer.) The certificate should have an expiration date, your con-tact information, and a description of the service. An example would be 4 square yards of custom quilting. If the quilt is larger or if the winner wants other services as well, then they will need to pay the dif-ference. Give the organizers of the auction an idea of what an appropriate minimum bid would be for your service.

Another way to donate your quilting service is by a specific dollar amount. If the guild has a door prize or raffle drawing, you could make up a certificate for $25 to $50 toward quilting or other services.

CHAPTER 8

Developing Your Quilting Style

As you learn to use your machine, start off with the easy techniques and add more as your confidence level increases. Some ways to speed up the learning process include taking classes, watching videos, and discussing ideas with other professional quilters. The costs of each of these educational tools are business expenses and are tax-deductible.

Classes and Videos

As a professional quilter, clients look to you for answers or guidance about everything quilt related.

Any class you take on piecing, storing quilts, washing quilts, attaching borders, and choosing quilting designs adds to your knowledge base. The more you educate yourself, the more you can educate your client. Check "Resources" on page 75 for online listings of classes, traveling teachers, video instruction, machine-quilters' conferences, and other ways to attend classes. Don't forget classes at your local quilt shops, quilt guilds, and retreats.

For more specialized and longer duration instruction, such as techniques applicable to your specific machine or your business, look into taking classes at the larger quilt and trade shows. Check with your machine dealer for trade shows specific to sewing machines, embroidery machines, machine quilting, and long-arm and short-arm machines.

International Machine Quilters Association (IMQA)

The IMQA is a professional association for machine quilters. Its trade show is called Machine Quilters Showcase and is held each year in the spring along with its annual meeting. As a member, you'll receive the association's quarterly newsletter, *On Track.* Check the "Resources" section for the Web site address, where you can find listings of regional associations of machine quilters.

Internet E-Mail Lists

One way to get a daily dose of machine-quilting information for your business and about your machine is to join an Internet e-mail list. Here you can "listen in on" and contribute to conversations as other professional quilters ask and answer questions about their businesses (and sometimes their personal lives). These lists are not strictly limited to machine quilting, but the majority of the e-mails do stay on that subject. Just hit the delete key if you are not interested in the subject of a particular e-mail.

Two Web sites that offer many different mailing lists are YahooGroups and Quiltropolis. (See "Resources" for Web site addresses.) These Web sites include lists specific to your sewing or quilting machine or specific techniques, such as appliqué and watercolor quilting. Each list has its own rules about posting advertisements or information for personal gain or personal or unrelated information. Read the information provided at the time you sign up.

Patterns and Books

More and more pattern designers are making patterns available to quilters for commercial use. By that, I mean some patterns can be used over and over in your business, resized as needed, without infringing upon someone's copyright. Be sure to check that the patterns you use give permission for using them in this way. Otherwise, copyright laws prohibit the commercial use of patterns. If you copy a pattern from a magazine or book, resize it, reproduce it, and use it in your business without permission, you are violating copyright laws. If you purchase patterns from professional quilting suppliers, they usually can be used and reproduced in your commercial business, but double-check to be sure.

Ideas for quilting designs are all around you. They are on wallpaper, in coloring books, and on floor tiles. If you see a design that inspires you, make a drawing of it. Later, you can play with it to see how you might make your own designs. Books and magazines are a more conventional source for design ideas. If you see how someone else quilted the background of an appliqué block, you might find that it would look great in the background of a pieced block. Often, you can add your own style and make freehand designs to fit your purposes. Practice by drawing your own designs either on paper or freehand with the machine.

Your Portfolio and Design Ideas

As you see designs that could inspire quilting patterns, draw them in a journal or notebook. Carry your notebook with you everywhere because you never know when a design idea might present itself. Quilt shops and quilt shows are good sources of ideas, as are magazines and books. Page through your notebook for inspiration when you need to plan your next quilting design.

Take several pictures of each completed quilt. Be sure to take close-up pictures of the quilting designs and make notes about how you planned, marked, and stitched the quilt. Make notes about anything you would do differently next time. If you completed a quilting plan or sketches for this quilt, put that information together with the pictures and your final notes. This design book becomes your professional portfolio that you can show to clients.

CHAPTER 9

Scheduling Your Time

One of the necessary evils of any business is scheduling. If you don't schedule your time and follow that schedule, you'll meet yourself coming and going. Like the old adage says, time is money, so wasting time in your business or spending it in inefficient ways wastes money. You may need to go through several variations of your schedule, but keep trying until you find one that works for you.

In this chapter you'll find suggestions for keeping a calendar, scheduling quilts, managing a waiting list, and keeping track of quilts in your care. These things are of the utmost importance because this is where you interact with your client. Don't cut corners when it comes to scheduling your time and keeping track of quilts.

When I first started in this business, I would take calls like this from customers: "Can you quilt a top for me?" they would ask. "Yes, bring it over tomorrow," I'd say. As my business increased, these calls became more and more frequent. One day, I realized that I wasn't getting much quilting or anything else done because I was constantly taking in quilts. At the end of the week, I would end up with more unquilted tops than I started with and I hadn't finished a single quilt to return. I had no idea when I would get to a particular client's quilt or which quilt I would work on next. I would find myself wondering "Didn't Mrs. Jones need that quilt for a wedding or something?" or "What did she say to quilt in that third border?"

When I had just a few clients, I could easily remember all those details without writing them down. But as my client list grew, it was time to get organized, keep good records, and make a plan that would work for me. The things I use to schedule my appointments are:

◆ A calendar that shows a week at a time. I like a calendar that has a line for each half or quarter hour between the hours of 8:00 A.M. and 6:00 P.M., but use whatever works best for you.

◆ A quilting planner/waiting list that lists the client name and phone number and has spaces for recording the drop-off date; notes about quilting, notification and pick-up dates; and spaces to check off when a quilt comes in or goes out. This form is discussed later; see "Maintaining a Waiting List" on page 61.

◆ An alphabetical address book

Each of these items is discussed below.

Using a Calendar

The first step in getting organized is to schedule on your calendar the events that you are aware of right now. You started this exercise earlier in chapter 1, when you went through the exercise of filling out your calendar and estimating the number of quilts you could complete each week.

Keep your calendar current by writing down even the most insignificant items or events as they come up. Look at your calendar at least once each day, even on the weekends. You might think you had the appointment time right without checking your calendar, until the client shows up an hour earlier than you expected! Listed below are some events and appointments to consider when filling out your calendar.

PERSONAL EVENTS

I consider personal business anything that is not directly related to my quilting business, such as school events, holidays, quilt shows, baseball games, dates with my spouse, doctor appointments, and housecleaning. In other words—life. Do yourself a favor and schedule in time for your own quilting or piecing. If you like to attend quilting bees and guild meetings, schedule those as well. Don't make the mistake of putting yourself last.

The events or appointments where you control the date and times should be scheduled when they are convenient for you. Doctor appointments, grocery shopping and going to the post office, doing housework and laundry, getting your hair cut and your nails manicured, these are all things you can schedule. I consider all of these things errands and try to schedule these on my designated errand day. Choose one day a week to get all these things done. Some weeks you will have just a few errands to run and other weeks you'll be running around all day. By designating an errand day, you limit the number of interruptions during the rest of the week.

Schedule as far ahead in this year or next as you have to. If you know when your children are off for spring break, write that down. The younger my kids were, the less work I got done while they were in the house. When they were on spring break, so was I. I didn't schedule any quilting time that week. Think ahead about vacations, weddings, quilt shows, classes, or anything else that can affect your workweek.

QUILTING DAYS

Now schedule days to devote to business quilting. Try to have as many of these days as you can and schedule them so you have little or no interruptions during those days. Don't schedule quilting time on errand days unless you have no errands for that day. The fewer interruptions you have, the faster you can complete each quilt. Include a few hours each week for doing paperwork that must be done.

DROP-OFF AND PICK-UP DAYS

These are days devoted to seeing clients. Try to limit client appointments to one day per week if you can. Often, clients are not available on your scheduled day and will need to come "after hours." For the most part, however, you should be able to devote one or two days a week to appointments for clients to drop off and pick up their quilts. On those days, the time between appointments might be times that you can set aside for paperwork, laundry, or even a little personal quilting or piecing.

My drop-off days are Thursday and Friday and I schedule appointments about an hour apart. This allows a little extra time for clients who might be early or ones who are running late. It also gives me time to put away the quilt I just took in or set up the quilt that is going home with the next client. When I have few or no appointments on those days, I can get a jump on some items from my errand list or I can tackle some more quilting, paperwork, or household chores.

REST DAYS

Here is where you can schedule some time for yourself and your family. The more things you have going on, the more you need a schedule. Include holidays, vacation days, and "mental-health" days when you just might need a break.

HOLIDAY RUSH

Just about every professional quilter I know is rushed during the holidays. There is so much going on during this stressful time, and clients want quilts to give as gifts. You have an opportunity to take advantage of the holiday rush and take in a few extra quilts—but be careful. If you don't schedule your time efficiently, you'll be too tired to enjoy the holiday. One year, I quilted all the way up to December 23 and did not get any shopping done. The next two days were hectic and before I knew it we were ringing in the New Year. Where was my holiday?

Now I stop quilting the day my kids go on break from school and don't start again until they return. I have a much more enjoyable holiday break, and we actually have time to make lasting memories. If you want a less stressful holiday, schedule your time off and enjoy yourself. You can prepare for the holiday rush by notifying clients early in the year that if they have holiday quilting, they need to schedule it early. If you don't celebrate holidays or don't require as much time off, then go ahead and schedule as much quilting as you can stand.

Scheduling Quilts

Now that you have filled in your calendar, you can schedule quilts for each week. In this example, we are limiting ourselves to three quilts per week. (Remember the scenario in chapter 1 where I calculated that it would take me an average of 7 hours per quilt and I had 21 hours available for quilting each week?) Open your calendar to the next week you have planned for quilting days. If there is a holiday or some other event that cuts into your quilting days, you will want to schedule fewer than three quilts for that week.

Somewhere on that calendar page, either at the top or the bottom, wherever you have room, write the number 1 with a line next to it, then the number 2 with a line next to it, and then the number 3 with a line next to it, as shown below.

If you want to schedule only two quilts for that week, simply write in spaces for numbers 1 and 2. Leave enough space between the lines to fill in the clients' names later. These lines written on your calendar indicate the number of quilts you plan to quilt during this week. Do this for each week on your calendar for the next several months.

PREPARE FOR THE NEXT DAY

After you complete a quilt and you have a little time left at the end of the day, consider loading your next top. Since the quilting design decisions are already made, you can complete the mundane task of loading the quilt without worrying about the quilting. Load the backing, batting, and top as you normally do and prepare the machine, thread, patterns, and bobbins as well. With the top already loaded and ready to go, you can start fresh the next morning and get right to the fun stuff. This makes good use of a small block of time left from the day before.

Look ahead to any tops for which you may need to purchase thread or batting or for which you need to prepare a pattern, and have these ready so you can start right in.

1 _____

2 _____   3 _____

Week of June 16

MONDAY, JUNE 16	TUESDAY, JUNE 17	WEDNESDAY, JUNE 18	THURSDAY, JUNE 19
7	7	7	7
:30	:30	:30	:30
8	8	8	8
:30	:30	:30	:30
9	9	9	9
:30	:30	:30	:30
10	10	10	10
:30	:30	:30	:30
11	11	11	11
:30	:30	:30	:30
12	12	12	
:30			

Maintaining a Waiting List

This form is a combination quilting planner, waiting list, and quilt tracker. Using this form together with your calendar lets you keep track of clients and their quilts. It consists of five columns:

Name and Phone Number. Record the client's name and telephone number so you have the contact information when needed.

Drop Off. This column should have room to record an appointment date and a space to check off when the quilt is received.

Quilt Week Of. Record the week you plan to work on this quilt.

Client Notified. Write down when you've called (or e-mailed) the client to notify him or her that the quilt is ready for pickup.

Pick Up. Like the "Drop-Off" column, you need space to record pick-up appointment dates and to check off when the quilt has been returned. See the sample Quilting Planner on page 65, which you can photocopy to use for your business.

The first information entered on this form falls under the column labeled "Quilt Week Of." This column is the beginning of your waiting list. On your calendar, go back to the first week that you scheduled quilts. Let's say that is the week of Monday, June 16. On your calendar, you have scheduled three quilts for that week by writing in line 1, line 2, and line 3. Under the column "Quilt Week Of," fill in a line for each of those three quilts. Write the date, such as June 16 (for the Monday of that week).

Your Quilting Planner should now have the first three lines filled in under "Quilt Week Of."

Go to the next week of your calendar, which is the week of Monday, June 23. During this week, you are attending a quilting retreat so you scheduled just one quilt for that week. Fill in just one line on the Quilting Planner under "Quilt Week Of" for June 23. Flip over to the next week, Monday, June 30. You have three quilts scheduled for that week. On your Quilting Planner under "Quilt Week Of," the next three lines are June 30. You now have seven lines filled out on your form, with all the information under one column, as shown below.

QUILTING PLANNER				
	Drop Off	✔	Quilt Week of	Client
			6-16	
			6-16	
			6-16	
			6-23	
			6-30	
			6-30	
			6-30	

At this point, you know that in the next three weeks you can quilt up to seven quilts for clients. If a client calls you right now and asks how soon you can quilt for them, all you need do is look at the Quilting Planner to see that the next available opening is the week of June 16.

Continue through as many months as you want to go, filling in the "Quilt Week Of" column. You will need more than one copy of this form, so number the pages to keep them in order. I keep my Quilting

Planner sheets in a three-ring binder with my address book. The binder is zippered and has a carrying handle. My weekly calendar is zippered inside the binder for traveling.

Scheduling Clients

Now that you have your waiting list started, you can begin filling in client information as they call. Mrs. Smith calls and asks when she can drop off a quilt. Look at your Quilting Planner to see that the first open entry under "Quilt Week Of" is June 16. You say that you can quilt her top the week of June 16. She agrees and you write her name and phone number on the first opening for the week of June 16.

The next step is to schedule the drop-off appointment, so ask Mrs. Smith when she would like to drop off her quilt top. I ask my clients to drop off their top the week before it is to be quilted. On your calendar, turn to the week before June 16 and find the days designated as drop-off/pick-up days and schedule the appointment on one of those days. If you set the drop-off appointment for June 12 at 1:30 P.M., write that appointment on your weekly calendar and in the drop-off column on the Quilting Planner. You have now scheduled Mrs. Smith to drop off her quilt the week before it is scheduled to be quilted and you have scheduled her top to be the first one quilted during the week of June 16.

Don't forget to also schedule Mrs. Smith's top on your calendar. Flip the calendar to the week of June 16 and on line 1, fill in Mrs. Smith's name. This tells you that during that week you have scheduled a quilt for Mrs. Smith. When June 16 actually arrives, you will know which top to pull out and quilt first that week. (See the sample charts on the facing page.)

If you are booked too far into the future to make appointments, then simply take the client's name and number and write it in the next available space under "Name and Phone." Even if you are booked 18 months into the future, you are still able to give the client a fairly good estimate of the week that you can quilt his or her top. As the time for their quilt approaches, call the client back to set up an appointment.

Tracking Quilts in Your Care

It is important for you to know exactly how many quilts you have in your studio at any given time. The Quilting Planner keeps track of this if you have filled it out properly. When Mrs. Smith comes to deliver her top, put a checkmark in the little box in the drop-off column. That tells you that Mrs. Smith's quilt top and other materials are in your possession.

When you have completed Mrs. Smith's quilt, give her a call to tell her that the quilt is ready to be picked up. Let's say you get her 15-year-old daughter, who takes a message and quickly brushes you off. What are the odds that your message will be delivered? To keep track of this call, write the date of the call under "Client Notified." If you leave a message, note it in that column as well. Sometimes clients forget, messages don't get delivered, or people are out of town. Most people want their quilts back as soon as possible. If they have not returned your call in a reasonable amount of time, you can assume that they didn't get the message. Call again and note the second call on your Quilting Planner.

The client will usually make a pick-up appointment at the same time that you tell them the quilt is

When a client calls to schedule quilting, be sure to mark this appointment in three places:
1) Write the client's name and telephone number on the Quilting Planner at your first opening, or write it into a later week chosen by the two of you.

QUILTING PLANNER

Name and Phone	Drop Off	✔	Quilt Week of	Client Notified	
Mrs. Smith 999-555-1236	6-11		6-16		
			6-16		

2) Write the drop-off appointment on your calendar.

Week of June 9

MONDAY, JUNE 9	TUESDAY, JUNE 10	WEDNESDAY, JUNE 11	THURSDAY, JUNE 12
7	7	7	7
:30	:30	:30	:30
8	8	8	8
:30	:30	:30	:30
9	9	9 Mrs. Smith	9
:30	:30	:30 999-555-1234	:30
10	10	10	10
:30		:30	

3) Write the client's name on your calendar for the week that you will be doing the quilting.

1 Mrs. Smith
2 _____ 3 _____

Week of June 16

MONDAY, JUNE 16	TUESDAY, JUNE 17	WEDNESDAY, JUNE 18	THURSDAY, JUNE 19
7	7	7	7
:30	:30	:30	:30
8	8	8	8
:30	:30	:30	:30
9	9	9	9
:30	:30	:30	:30
10	10	10	10
:30		:30	

ready. Look at your calendar for the next available pick-up days and make an appointment for one of those days. Write the appointment on your calendar and on your Quilting Planner under "Pick Up." Now when you look at your Quilting Planner, you will see that Mrs. Smith's quilt is finished, she knows it, and she has made an appointment to pick it up. The only space not filled in on Mrs. Smith's line on the Quilting Planner is the check box under "Pick Up."

After Mrs. Smith has left with her quilt and you have payment in hand, check the box under "Pick Up." You have completed the entire process for Mrs. Smith.

If you want to know how many quilts you have at a given time, you can simply look at your Quilting Planner. All the rows that are completely filled out mean that you no longer have that quilt. If you have rows partially filled in, then look for the checkmarks under "Drop Off." Checkmarks under this column mean that you still have the quilt. The sample Quilting Planner below shows that there are two quilts in your studio. These quilts belong to Mrs. Jones and Mrs. Green.

One important thing to remember about the Quilting Planner is that you'll want to list each quilt top separately, as shown for Pam Nelson below. Remember that you are scheduling the number of quilts you can complete in a given week, so you need to keep track of quilt tops, not simply the number of clients.

QUILTING PLANNER						
Name and Phone	Drop Off	✔	Quilt Week of	Client Notified	Pick Up	
Mrs. Smith 999-555-1236	6-11		6-16	6-18	6-20	✔
Mrs. Jones 999-555-4321	6-12	✔	6-16			
Mrs. Green 999-555-2345	6-13	✔	6-16			
Mrs. Brown 999-555-4545	6-20		6-23			
Mrs. White 999-555-3621	6-20		6-30			
Pam Nelson 999-555-4822			6-30			
Pam Nelson 999-555-4822			6-30			

QUILTING PLANNER

Name and Phone	Drop Off	✔	Quilt Week of	Client Notified	Pick Up	✔

CHAPTER 10

Working with Clients

Conduct yourself in a businesslike manner every time you meet or talk with a client. If you appear scatterbrained or unsure of yourself or if you are not taking your business seriously, people will take their business elsewhere. In the beginning, clients might ask questions that you don't have answers to right away. Instead of telling them you just don't know, tell them that you will check into it and get back to them. This gives you a chance to do research or figure estimates so that you can give them an informed answer.

You want to exude confidence in yourself and your abilities without appearing to be a know-it-all. If a client asks for a particular type of quilting that you have not yet tried, tell them that you have not done it before but you would like to try it out. Assure them that you will not be practicing on their quilt but on a practice piece. Instead of making up a price on the spot if someone asks you to do a service that you normally don't do, tell them that you will get back to them with an estimate. Just because they asked doesn't mean that you must answer on the spot.

CLIENT CONFIDENTIALITY

As a professional, it is important that you treat your clients professionally. Even though you are under no legal obligation to keep conversations with your client confidential, you have a moral obligation to do so. Here are some Do's and Don'ts for keeping client information confidential.

- ◆ Don't name-drop. You shouldn't mention the names of any of your clients to anyone else. Leave it up to the client to let others know of the professional relationship between the two of you. If you want a list of references to give out, ask your clients if you can use their names for references before giving out names and contact information.
- ◆ Don't show a client's quilt to someone else without his or her permission. If you would like to take the quilt to show-and-share, ask first. And by no means show a quilt to another client before the owner has seen it.
- ◆ Do ask the client if you can take a picture of his or her quilt for your portfolio. If you wish to use that picture elsewhere, such as on your Web site, ask for permission to do so before you use it.
- ◆ Don't share information about a client or spread gossip around. It will come back to haunt you!

Your Reputation

I want to address the old adage that "the customer is always right" and how that affects your style, your technique, your reputation, and your business. The following example is food for thought as to how you might handle this or similar situations that arise in your business.

Let's say that your client brings in a beautifully appliquéd quilt top that clearly cries out for custom quilting. The mostly purple and pink flowers with different shades of green leaves are appliquéd on a light-colored background. You are perfectly capable of stitching beautiful custom quilting that will truly enhance the appearance of the top. However, the client wants to save a few dollars and demands that you put an allover cloud design over the entire quilt. And since her favorite color is purple, she wants you to use dark purple thread. What do you do?

Of course, this is a highly unlikely situation, but in cases where the client suggests a quilting method or choice of thread that reflects negatively on your work and reputation, encourage them to look at the alternatives. And if the client insists that you quilt the top her way, are you prepared to refuse this quilt top to protect your reputation?

If you quilt the top as the customer wants, this top will go out into the general public. Her family and quilting friends will see it. It may be displayed at the show-and-share segment of a few guild meetings, and it may even hang in some local quilt shows. When your client mentions you as the quilter, those who see it will judge your work by this quilt. Is this how you want people to view your work? Does it send the right message? What if the client receives negative comments about the quilting design, choice of thread color, or both? Will your client admit to her friends that it was her choice, not yours? What does this do to your reputation?

Over time, you will gain a reputation of making good suggestions and producing quality work without compromising your style or technique. Like other professionals, such as doctors, attorneys, and accountants, you are known by your name and reputation. And like other artists, you are known by the quilting you complete. Once your work leaves your place of business, you have no control over who sees it or how the client conveys his or her feelings about it. Your work is an indication of your abilities and must speak for itself. You cannot separate the two.

I have not had to refuse a quilt on this or similar grounds, but I have told clients that I am not comfortable doing something that neither the client nor I would be happy with the results. Fortunately, this approach has been enough to convince the client to choose another alternative.

Telephone Checklist and Journal

When taking calls from clients, especially when your business is new, it is good to have a checklist next to the telephone and a journal to record any notes. The checklist could be a copy of your service order or brochure and should cover subjects such as batting, thread, quilting designs, and backing fabric. The checklist is used to remind you what you need to talk about with the client. Be sure to cover any policies you may have, such as how much larger to make the backing and batting and options for pressing the quilt top.

Keep a daily business journal that includes information about business conversations with vendors and clients, along with any problems you had and how you solved them. Write the date at the top of the page and jot down notes when someone calls or something happens that you want to remember. When talking to clients, some of these notes might include the size of the quilt, the piecing pattern, and any questions the client may have that you can check on later. If you give them a cost estimate, write that

down as well. The daily business journal has helped me out more than a few times and has been invaluable in my business.

Drop-Off Appointment

When it's time for the client to arrive, be prepared. Be sure you know his or her name so you can use it when greeting the client. Nothing is more embarrassing than to greet someone at your door and not know his or her name! I take a blank service order and write the client's name and phone number(s) at the top. For a service order you can photocopy for your business use, see page 74.

Make sure the room where you meet is clean and neat and all pets are elsewhere for the time being. To avoid unpleasant odors, you might want to put off cooking until the client is gone. Open up some windows or light a candle to make the house smell fresh.

Some things to have ready are a measuring tape for measuring the quilt, a calculator, service order or other paper, pen, your portfolio, and any thread or pattern samples you might need. Refer to your business journal for any comments you wrote regarding this client. Have one of your brochures and/or business cards to give the client.

Make sure you have a place for the client to sit to discuss the quilt. Remove anything from sight that you do not want them to see, such as personal belongings, shoes, newspapers, and bills. For quite a while, I had my clients sit on one side of the table. One evening, I sat in the client chair and the only thing to look at was my kitchen! Now I direct them to the opposite chair so they can look at my ceramic pitcher collection on the baker's rack. This view is much more pleasant for them and I don't have to worry about them seeing what I'm having for dinner that evening.

Turn the television off and either have no noise or music playing softly. Make the visit pleasant for the client but not so pleasant they want to stay and visit for a while. Keep the conversation on the quilting, and a typical drop-off visit should last no more than 15 to 20 minutes.

Service Order

A service order can be as complicated or as simple as you want. With my word-processing software and computer, I print my own service order to use for each quilt. By using a service order, you can be sure to cover each subject during the drop-off appointment. If you feel it is necessary, you can include your policies or any disclaimers you want the client to be aware of and/or a place for the client to sign.

At the very least, you should have one piece of paper for each quilt top. It should include the client's name and telephone number, the quilt size, and the type of quilting ordered. The service order reminds you what your prices are. If you forget to charge the client for a service, then you have lost that income. If, after the drop-off appointment, you notice you forgot to charge a client for a service, let them know that normally you charge for that service but you neglected to add it to their order. That way, they'll be aware that the next time they order that particular service there will be a charge for it. I call these kinds of mistakes "tuition" because it costs you to learn something!

In the following sections, I explain all the entries on the sample service order. Your service order should include your prices and your services.

CLIENT

The first blank line on the form is for the client name and phone number. Fill this out before the client arrives and have the form ready. Later, when you go over the completed service order with the client, confirm that you have the correct work and/or home phone numbers. Use the space at the top of the form to write any extra information that applies to that particular quilt top or client. Some of this information might include a particular completion date, a note to remind you not to leave a message on the answering machine because the quilt is a gift, or information that the client will be out of town when the quilt is completed.

QUILT

List the measurements of the quilt top and calculate the surface area that you use for pricing. (See "Determining Quilting Time per Surface Area" on page 36). If you are attaching bindings and you charge by the inch or foot, then calculate the perimeter of the quilt top and fill in that number.

QUILTING

The next two sections have to do with the quilting. Allover designs are listed first, along with the fee to remind you of what you charge. I've left the fee area blank on the form so you may photocopy it if you'd like. Make one copy, fill in your fees, and then make multiple copies.

Calculate the charge and enter the number in the space. List the quilting design or pattern chosen. The custom quilting section has spaces for block, sashing, and border designs, as well as a special instructions section. Calculate the cost for the custom quilting and enter it on the line. Fill in all information about the quilting and include thread colors if necessary. If you charge extra for different items of custom quilting, list those on your service order. If you charge extra for turning a quilt or for setting in borders or blocks, be sure to include a space for that charge on your form.

Often, I will use the back of the service order to sketch out ideas for the client. If they don't choose an idea, cross it out so you won't be confused later. If they choose a sketched design, I put a note by it indicating where it is to be quilted and which color thread to use. In the "Custom Quilting" section, write "Over" or some other reminder to yourself to look at the back of the service order. With this method, you have the actual quilting design sketched out for your client to see and for you to follow while quilting. Custom quilting can get very involved, with different designs and thread changes, so make sure all the information is clearly written.

THREAD

The thread-color section is a place to write information about thread usage. The sample service order shows a flat thread rate of $6 for each quilt and that number is already filled in. You may wish to include the cost of thread in your regular quilting fee, or to charge more for decorative or specialty threads as an alternative.

BATTING

The batting section is the place to indicate the client's batting choice. There is a separate line to list the brand of batting furnished by the client. This is important if you have several clients who all furnish batting in different brands and you have their quilt tops at the same time. You will know which batting belongs to which client. On your service order, list any battings you sell and the price for each.

BACKING

The backing is listed in case you get requests to seam, press, or square up the backing. If you sell backings, include a line for that charge.

BINDING

I list all the different steps involved in completing a binding because not every client wants me to do each stage of binding. Some clients bring the already-prepared binding to be attached. Others want me to prepare and attach the binding for them so they can stitch it by hand. Some bring a yard of fabric and ask me to do the whole thing. I found it easiest to list and charge for each step separately according to the services requested.

TOTALS

The last section of the form is for totaling the charges and applying whatever taxes or fees you are required to collect. After completing the service order, go over each item again with the client so you both have a clear understanding of the services you are being asked to render. The service order should be kept together with the quilt, backing, batting, binding, or whatever the client brings. Most often, the client will bring the top and backing in some sort of bag. In most cases, the completed quilt will not fit in this bag so if the bag is of no use to you, send it home with the client.

After the quilting is completed, save each service order and file it by date or customer name, because you'll have repeat clients who like what you did on their quilt but can't remember exactly what was done. If you have their prior service order, you can refer to it later. The service order can be used as a record of income as well. A sample completed service order is shown on the facing page.

Service Order

Name _Jane Brown_   Telephone _999-555-4545_

Quilt Size _87 x 93_   Square Yards _6.2_   Perimeter _360_

- -

Allover Quilting ($_____ / square yard) $ _____

Design _____

- -

Custom Quilting ($_40_ / square yard) $_248_

Block Design _Feather Wreath_   Sashing Design _____

Border Design _Diagonal Grid with Cream_

Special Instructions _Center backing if possible._
SID blocks with clear

- -

Thread Color _above_ $ 6.00

Batting _____ Client Furnished (Brand) _____

____ Cotton ($_____ / inch)   ____ Poly ($_____ / inch)   ✓ 80-20 ($_.32_ / inch) $_31.04_

Backing   Number of Seams _____ $ _____

     Square up ($25.00) _____   Press ($25.00) _____ $ _____

Binding _____ Prepare ($.08/inch)   _____ Attach ($.04/inch)

     _____ Machine Finish ($.04/inch)   _____ Hand Finish ($.08/inch) $ _____

- -

                            Subtotal $_285.04_

        _8.25%_   Tax $_23.52_

                               Total $_308.56_

Pick-Up Appointment

Pick-up appointments are usually quick, under 15 minutes, so it's safe to schedule these at 30-minute intervals. As with the drop-off appointment, be prepared before the client arrives. Have the quilt displayed so the client can see it right away. (See "Display Stand" on page 23.) Have the invoice or receipt and a pen ready for check writing. After the client is finished admiring the completed quilt, take it down and fold it while he or she is writing the check.

Mail-Order Business

If you will be doing business through the mail, you will not have face-to-face contact with your clients. When they ship their quilts through the mail or other shipping service, these are the steps you can follow:

◆ Get as much information over the telephone or via e-mail as you can.

◆ Ask clients to let you know when they ship and what carrier to expect. If you have a preference for carriers, ask them to use that carrier (if, for example, you know that a certain carrier is more reliable with delivery times). The fabric (and batting if they're providing it) should be placed inside a plastic bag and then into the box. The plastic bag protects the fabric should the box get wet. The box should be large enough to hold the completed quilt, so you may want to furnish a minimum size. This saves you from having to get a larger box to ship it back.

◆ Call clients the day their quilts are received to let them know they arrived safely. Before you call, determine some recommendations for quilting. As you discuss the quilting, fill out the service order and determine the price. Prices should include any shipping and insurance charges. Ask clients to send their checks in time to arrive the week their quilts are completed.

◆ Notify clients when you are shipping quilts back to them so they can be on the lookout or make other arrangements if they'll be out of town.

Other Considerations

There are many things that you need to discuss with your clients, and as you gain experience, those things will become part of your routine. Experience helps you become more efficient, and things that once caused setbacks should not happen again. Below are some things that have made me lose time or caused me to have a red face! Hopefully, they won't happen to you.

CREATIVE CONTROL

Sometimes clients will be very specific about how they want their tops quilted, or perhaps you have suggested something you thought would look nice. However, when you start to actually do the quilting, you realize that the look is not what you expected, the color is not right, or the piecing and quilting are fighting each other. If this happens, you will have a loaded, partially quilted quilt on your frame. In cases like this, you should call the client, describe the situation, and determine a new plan. When you call a client, be sure to have recommendations ready.

If the client is out of town, shopping, in the hospital, or otherwise unavailable to discuss the problem, you cannot go on until a decision is made. You must either wait it out or unload the quilt and begin another. Waiting costs you time and taking the quilt off the frame risks creating puckers when it is reloaded.

To make sure this does not happen, make it your policy to have creative control over any changes to the designs that were previously agreed upon. If you can anticipate possible problems, discuss alternatives with the client beforehand. If your policy is to have creative control, inform your clients of this before they leave quilts with you.

SHEETS FOR BACKING

Occasionally, you will have a client that buys a bed sheet on sale to use as a quilt backing. If you have discussed backings before the appointment and they mention to you that they are using a sheet, ask them to wash the sheet before bringing it to you because there might be a problem with stitch quality due to the sizing in the sheet. Ask them to remove all the hems and be sure the remaining part of the sheet is large enough for the quilt top.

BATTING AND FABRIC SCRAPS

You might be tempted to keep scraps of fabric and batting that you have trimmed from your client's quilts. Please don't do this. Those scraps belong to the client and should be returned to them. If the scrap is smaller than 2" wide, I usually toss it. But if it is wider than 2", it gets folded and returned to the client. Some people keep close track of what they bring to you and they might have a designated use for the scraps they expect to get back, such as a hanging sleeve to coordinate with the backing. If you are collecting batting scraps to use or to give away, ask your clients if they would mind giving you the scraps for these purposes.

NO PAYMENT, NO QUILT!

The majority of your clients will have no problem paying for their quilt at pick-up time. However, you will occasionally have a client who'll ask if they can pay you later or who have forgotten their checkbooks or money. Make it clear to them that you are happy to keep their quilt until they can pay for it. Never let a quilt leave your studio without first receiving payment.

JUST ONE ROW

During the course of your quilting business, you will come across clients with a wide range of piecing, appliqué, and design skills. This means that not all quilts are perfectly pieced and not all quilts are fun to look at. Each of us has different tastes, and beauty is in the eye of the beholder.

You will occasionally receive a quilt top that, although lovingly made with quality fabrics and perfect piecing, will be boring to quilt. These quilts are usually very large, king-size quilts of one block design and about three fabrics. When I get a quilt like this, I must force myself to work on it. Quilting each block in each row is monotonous and seems to be endless. These are usually the large quilts that are custom quilted so there is a large sum of money due when quilting is complete.

How I handle these large, boring jobs is to quilt just one row at a time. Usually I quilt one or two rows, then stop to do something else for about 15 to 30 minutes. This is actually a good time to do some stretching exercises, pay a few bills, or plan the next week's meals. I actually look at the clock and tell myself what time to return. After this short break, I return to quilt another row or two. It takes longer to complete the quilt, but psychologically I can handle it better. Before I know it, the boring task is done and I am ready for the next quilt.

Service Order

Name _____ Telephone _____

Quilt Size _____ Square Yards _____ Perimeter _____

- -

Allover Quilting ($_____ / square yard) $ _____

Design _____

- -

Custom Quilting ($_____ / square yard) $ _____

Block Design _____ Sashing Design _____

Border Design _____

Special Instructions _____

_____

- -

Thread Color _____ $ 6.00

Batting _____ Client Furnished (Brand) _____

_____ Cotton ($_____ / inch)   _____ Poly ($_____ / inch)   _____ 80-20 ($_____ / inch) $ _____

Backing   Number of Seams _____ $ _____

      Square up ($25.00) _____   Press ($25.00) _____ $ _____

Binding   _____ Prepare ($.08/inch)   _____ Attach ($.04/inch)

      _____ Machine Finish ($.04/inch)   _____ Hand Finish ($.08/inch) $ _____

- -

Subtotal $ _____

Tax $ _____

Total $ _____

Resources

Whether you're just getting started with a quilting system or you've been doing it a while and are now ready to turn your hobby into a profession, the vendors listed here can help you reach your goals.

Tabletop Quilting Systems

The Grace Company
PO Box 27823
Salt Lake City, UT 84127
Toll-free: 800-264-0644
Phone: 801-485-6688
E-mail: info@graceframe.com
Web site: www.graceframe.com

HandiQuilter Inc.
322 E. 500 North
Centerville, UT 84014
Phone: 801-292-7988
E-mail: sales@handiquilter.com
Web site: www.handiquilter.com

Pennywinkle Valley Ranch
1695 Pennywinkle Branch Road
Waverly, TN
Phone: 931-296-5067
E-mail: pennywinkle@earthlink.net
Web site: www.pennywinklevalleyranch.com

Super Quilter
CSM Ltd.
1730 McPherson Court, Unit 15
Pickering, ON
Canada L1W 3E5
Phone: 877-837-5557
E-mail: info@superquilter.com
Web site: www.superquilter.com

Long-Arm Quilting Systems

A-1 Quilting Machines
3232 Evans Road
Springfield, MO 65804
Toll-free: 800-LONG-ARM (800-566-4276)
E-mail: a1qm@aol.com
Web site: www.long-arm.com

American Professional Quilting Systems
8033 University Avenue, Suite F
Des Moines, IA 50325
Toll-free: 800-426-7233 (U.S. and Canada)
Phone: 515-267-1113
E-mail: apqs@netins.net
Web site: www.apqs.com

Gammill Quilting Machine Company

1452 West Gibson Street
West Plains, MO 65775
Toll-free: 800-659-8224
   (U.S. and Canada)
Phone: 417-256-5919
E-mail: Gammill@townsqr.com
Web site: www.gammill.net

Intellistitch

Kasa Engineering Services
3023 Leatherlips Trail
Dublin, OH 43017
Phone/Fax: 614-792-0501
E-mail:
   zoltan@kasaengineering.com
Web site: www.intellistitch.com

KenQuilt Manufacturing

121 Pattie Street
Wichita, KS 67211
Toll-free: 866-784-5872
Phone: 316-303-0880
E-mail: sales@kenquilt.com
Web site: www.kenquilt.com

Nolting Longarm Quilting Machines

1265 Hawkeye Drive
Hiawatha, IA 52233
Phone: 319-378-0999
E-mail: nolting@nolting.com
Web site: www.nolting.com

Nustyle Quilting Machine & Supplies

309 W. 4th, Highway 52
Stover, MO 65078
Phone: 573-377-2244
E-mail: nustyle@advertisnet.com

Prodigy Machine Corporation

1310 W. Main Street
Rock Hill, SC 29732
Phone: 803-327-2121
E-mail: cpresler@rhtc.net
Web site: www.prodigyquilter.com

Statler Stitcher

700 W. Route K
Columbia, MO 65203
Phone: 573-449-1068
E-mail: paul@statlerstitcher.com
Web site: www.statlerstitcher.com

Supplies and Accessories

Most dealers and representatives offer a full line of supplies and notions, including instructional videos.

A Quilter's Studio

2418 S. Tyler Avenue
Joplin, MO 64804
Toll-free: 866-781-8550
Fax: 417-781-1965
E-mail: Liton43@aol.com
Web site:
   www.aquiltersstudio.com

Columbia River Quilting & Designs

1920 NE 149th Avenue
Vancouver, WA 98684
Phone: 360-892-2730
E-mail:
   dan@columbiariverquilting.com
Web site:
   www.columbiariverquilting.com

King's Men Quilting Supply, Inc.

2570 N. Walnut
Rochester, IL 62563
Toll-free: 888-744-0070
Phone: 217-498-9460
Fax: 217-498-9476
E-mail: dtaft@aol.com
Web site:
   www.kmquiltingsupply.com

Instruction and Teachers

Most dealers and representatives offer a full line of supplies and notions, including instructional videos.

Darlene Epp

Trillium House Longarm Training
   Centre
4397 Atwood Crescent
Abbotsford, BC
Canada V3G 2Y7
Phone: 604-850-5066
E-mail: depp@attcanada.ca
Web site:
   www.longarmsupplies.com

Innovations: A Machine Quilting Conference
PO Box 58335
Renton, WA 98058
Phone: 253-854-3362
Web site:
www.mqinnovations.com

Quilt University
www.quiltuniversity.com

Cindy Roth
Longarm University
12313 SE 198th Street
Renton, WA 98058
Phone: 253-854-3362
Fax: 253-854-0463
E-mail: longarmu@aol.com
Web site:
www.longarmuniversity.com

Sherry D. Rogers
Runway Ranch Longarm Quilting
Services
19702 8th Avenue South
Des Moines, WA 98148
Phone: 206-412-4720
Web site:
www.sewfarsewgood.org

Machine Quilters Showcase
International Machine Quilters
Association, Inc.
Web site: www.imqa.org

Marcia Stevens
Little Pine Studio
218 N. 10th Street
Brainerd, MN 56401
Phone: 218-828-9116
E-mail: mstevens@brainerd.net

Publications and Organizations

International Machine Quilters Association, Inc.
Web site: www.imqa.org

The Professional Quilter
Professional Quilter Publications
22412 Rolling Hill Lane
Laytonsville, MD 20882
E-mail:
info@professionalquilter.com
Web site:
www.professionalquilter.com

Unlimited Possibilities
Little Pine Studio
218 N. 10th Street
Brainerd, MN 56401-3420
Phone: 218-828-9116
E-mail: mstevens@brainerd.net

Software

Intuit
Web site: www.intuit.com

QuickStart
Bona Robinson
400 Sunset Drive
Baden, PA 15005
Phone: 724-935-3167
E-mail: bonajr@aol.com

Quilt Bags and Hangers

Atlanta Thread
Phone: 770-389-9115
Web site: www.atlantathread.com

Bags and Bows
33 Union Avenue
Sudbury, MA 01776
Toll-free: 800-225-8155
Fax: 800-225-8455
Web site:
www.bagsandbowsonline.com

Paper Mart
Toll-free: 800-745-8800
Web site: www.papermart.com

Uline Inc.
2200 S. Lakeside Drive
Waukegan, IL 60085
Toll-free: 800-958-5463
Fax: 800-295-5571
E-mail:
Customer.service@uline.com
Web site: www.uline.com

Quilt Display Stand

Icon USA
Web site: www.iconusa.com

About the Author

Carol A. Thelen is the author of *Long-Arm Machine Quilting: The Complete Guide to Choosing, Using, and Maintaining a Long-Arm Machine*. She runs a successful machine-quilting service and teaches classes and lectures on machine, long-arm, and tabletop quilting; how to run a quilting business; and patchwork.

Carol lives in Pearland, Texas, with her husband and two children.

Index

accessories, 22
accounting, 15–16, 18
advertising, 48, 51–53
allover quilting, 40–41
appointments
    drop-off, 59, 68–69
    pick-up, 59, 72

backing, sheets as, 73
backing, 46–47
bags for finished quilts, 24
banking, 18
basting, 32, 45, 47
batting, 21, 38
binding, 45
bobbins, 20
bookkeeping software, 18
books and patterns, 55
borders, set-in, 42
brochures, 50–51
burrs, smoothing, 20
business and home life, planning,
    30, 58–59
business cards, 50
business entities, types of,
    25–26

calendar, 58–59
camera, 23
chairs, 22
check springs, 19

checklists, 68
child care, 27–28
classes, 54–55
clients
    definition of, 5
    scheduling, 62
    working with, 66–73
    comfort aids, 22
computer equipment, 17–18
confidentiality, 67
continuous-curve quilting, 44
copyright, 55
corporations, 26
costing. *See* pricing
costs, 6–7, 13–14
CPAs, 15–16
creative control, 72–73
custom quilting, 33, 41
customers, defined, 5
cutting tools, 20–21

design ideas, 55–56
display stand, 23
donations, 52–53

echo quilting, 43
edges, 47
education, 54–55
efficiency, 33, 39
emery cord, 20

employees, 28
expenses, 6–7, 13–24

fees, setting. *See* pricing
floor pads, 22
forms
    quilting planner, 65
    service order, 74
    timing chart, 32
free-form quilting, 41–42

goals, 7
grid quilting, 44
guilds, 51–52

health concerns, 29–30
holidays, scheduling, 59
home and business life, planning,
    27–30, 58–59

IMQA (International Machine
    Quilters Association), 55
income, estimating, 6–12
income taxes, 15–16
inspiration, 55–56
insurance, 16–17, 23
International Machine Quilters
    Association (IMQA), 55
Internet, 18, 52, 55
isolation, 27

labels, quilt, 47
licenses and permits, 14–16
lighting, 19
limited liability companies (LLCs), 26
loading time, 32
Long-Arm Machine Quilting, 19, 47

machine, timing of, 19
magazines, advertising in, 52
mail-order business, 72
marketing, 48–53
market research, 7
marking, time to complete, 32
meander quilting, 41
measurements, 34
mileage, recording, 14
monofilament, 22
motivation, 29

notions, 20

organization, 23, 68–74
outline quilting, 43

paperwork, 24, 69–71
partnerships, 26
parts, spare, 19
pattern motifs, 42
patterned meander quilting, 41–42
patterns and books, 55
payment policy, 73
permits and licenses, 14–16
photographing quilts, 23
physical concerns, 22, 29–30
pins and scissors, 20
planning. *See* scheduling
portfolio, 56
pressing services, 46
pressing tools, 20–21
pricing
    options, 10, 31–32
    timing tasks, 32–39
    See also specific services
professionalism, 66–68

Quicken (software), 18
quilting
    project scheduling, 59–62
    time, 32–33, 36–37
    types of, 40–44
Quilting Planner (form), 65
quilts
    photographing, 23
    storing, 19
    time to complete, 9–10
    tracking in-house, 62–65
quilt shops, working with, 48–50
quilt shows, 51

referrals, 7, 49–50
reputation, 67–68
research, 7
resources, list of, 75–77
retail vs. wholesale prices, 15

scheduling
    drop-off appointments, 59, 68–69
    importance of, 57
    pick-up appointments, 59, 72
    quilt projects, 59–62
    time for work, 8–12
    time off, 59
    with a calendar, 58–59
scissors and pins, 20
scraps, 73
service orders, 69–71
services to offer, determining, 40–47
sewing machines, 20
sheets as backing, 73
size of quilt, calculating, 34
software, bookkeeping, 18
sole proprietorships, 26
solitude, 27
spare parts, 19
stands, display, 23
stipple quilting, 41

stitching in the ditch, 42–43
storage of quilts, 19
studio space, 49–50
supplies and tools
    cutting and pressing, 20–21
    office, 17–18
    quilting, 19–24
switches, 19

taxes, 14–16, 26
telephone checklists, 68
telephone service, 18
thread, 22
time
    appointment scheduling, 62–64
    availability for business, 8–12
    managing, 57–59
    project scheduling, 59–62
    tracking tasks, 31–33
time off, scheduling, 59
timing tool, 19
tools. *See* supplies and tools
tracking
    quilts in-house, 62–65
    time spent on tasks, 31–33
trapunto, 44
trimming edges, 47

unloading time, 33

vacation time, 59

waiting lists, 61–62
wholesale vs. retail prices, 15

zoning, 16